ESSAYS ON CREATING REALITY

BOOK 6

FREDERICK DODSON

COPYRIGHT

DISCLAIMER

The author is not responsible for effects readers have or allegedly have from this book, just like a driving school instructor is not responsible for his students driving. Furthermore, the information provided in this book is not a substitute for conventional medical assistance.

CONTENTS

Foreword

These are collected articles written in 2020 and 2021. The rang of topics is broader than ever: Social Psychology, Man-Made Flying Saucers, the law of attraction, entity-possession and false-flag terror, just to name a few. You will notice that the articles on Covid, even though outdated, accurately predict what later happened.

Enjoy,

Frederick Dodson

1

For More Success, Ignore Mainstream Advice

For more success, ignore mainstream advice. For more happiness, avoid the crowds.

Today I am going on a weeklong vacation. I chose this day, because everyone else's January vacation has come to an end. Streets, Hotels and Mountain Slopes are crowd-free and it will be *wonderful*.

Why are there traffic jams? Because "everyone" leaves work around the same time. A more *flexible s*ociety would let people start and end their work whenever they like. When I employ people for jobs, I never tell them *when* to work. It's none of my business. Nor *how* to work. None of my business! I just give them the **outcome desired** and how much I'll pay for it. And by when I want the result. The details are up to them. If mainstream companies were run this way, it would appear chaotic, but it would get much more done.

I don't follow the mainstream, because that's the stuff "everybody" says and does. The reasoning is simple: 99% of the population are not all that rich, healthy and successful. That means the advice they followed is not that good.

Does this mean I'm a misanthrope? No. I realize that *most people* have good intentions with their advice. Parents who give their kids bad advice do so out of love. Their intentions are pure, but the mind is easily programmed with false information. The Ego naively believes whatever it picks up.

Most people think that a "package vacation" is a good idea. But is it really a good idea to wade through crowded airports, roads and beaches to finally get sunburned and drunk? Aren't there more rejuvenating experiences to be had at a lower cost?

Where do people end up who follow mainstream advice?

Contrast that with the beautiful, near-empty beaches you see me at in my videos.

The advice of "most people" is to "get a job". I was told so early on. After about 7 years of "having jobs," I realized that employment was helping the employer succeed, not myself. So I became self-employed and more successful. That's 7 years of my life wasted thanks to "mainstream advice". My success started when I began ignoring what I had been told.

I was told I need to go to College if I want a good job. But *most people* I knew, who had gone to College, were in debt and unemployed. Maybe College wasn't the only answer anymore. And it wasn't "a job" I was looking for, but a career, a life purpose. The advice should not be "get a job", it should be "discover your life purpose"! And you might be better off learning-by-doing, than sitting in a room hearing someone else lecture.

There is no end to the madness of crowds. Do you think that if Covid-19 had never been reported, anyone would notice that it exists?

The mis-education of people is driven by *mass* media, which I have been avoiding since 30 years. If you favor accurate information, I recommend you avoid it too. It is made by less than successful people for less than successful people.

The reality, in my view, is that eggs neither lower nor heighten your risk of diabetes. Human Beings just want to have something to talk about continually, so they make up stories. The mind continually makes up stories and our media is a reflection of that.

Here's a more recent example of mainstream delusion:

News | Julian Assange

Trump slammed for failing to pardon Assange, Snowden

The WikiLeaks founder and NSA whistleblower, seen by many as free-speech icons, were not included in outgoing US president's list of people being pardoned.

How dumb do you have to be, not to know that a U.S. President cannot pardon a non-U.S. Citizen who has never been convicted on U.S. Soil? And yet, in January 2021, the world's crowds chanted for Julian Assange to "be pardoned" by the President.

How much time and energy was wasted trying to get Assange "pardoned" by Trump? Had I made a twitter post saying "Assange can't be pardoned by President Trump because he was not convicted in the U.S." I'd have mainstreamers respond: *"So you are* against *pardoning Assange? What kind of idiot are you?"* or *"So you are* for *pardoning Assange? What kind of idiot are you?"*. But I didn't say whether I am for or against freeing Assange, did I? Such can be the madness of crowds and the reason I don't bother commenting on most "current events".

For the record, I favor *freeing* Assange. Journalism is in such a dire state (see images above), because we have locked up genuine truth-tellers.

I'd go so far as to say that every success I have ever had came from doing the opposite of mainstream advice, of going against the crowd.

Mainstream advice told me to find a partner similar to me. I looked for a partner different from me and found happiness.

Mainstream advice told me to buy a house and live in it. I bought a house and rented it out and found financial gain.

Mainstream advice gave us the following food pyramid in the 1980s and 1990s. Ever since I do **the exact opposite** of it (except for the sweets), my health is perfect.

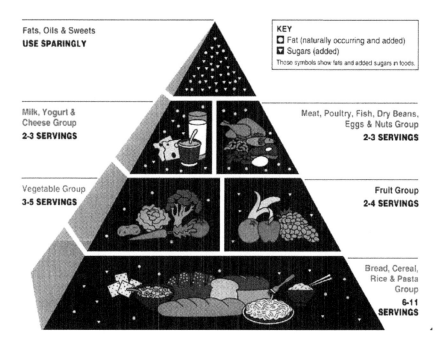

Could it be that this kind of advice, put out by the U.S. Department of Agriculture, was put out because the U.S. has an excess of wheat and somehow needs a market for it? Is "mainstream advice" susceptible to special financial interests, and therefore questionable? That's something to ponder.

If I do not follow mainstream advice, then what? 1) Research and 2) Listening to the Heart. Research means to study a subject before making major decisions on it. And listening to the heart means to become silent and feel. The heart is uninfluenced by peer pressure, current "trends", parents, school, media, history–the external world. How do I really feel about a thing? About a choice? About a person? About a path? Such an important question. Don't let how you really feel be drowned out by the noise of the crowds. Your soul is not of this Earth and has a different viewpoint. You are in the world, but not of it. And if you wish your life to be a fantastic success, listen to your heart.

2

That Magical Flow State Where Time Slows Down And Space Stretches

The amazing state of flow, where **t i m e** slows down and **s p a c e** stretches. How many more times will I write about this? Many more! I'll write a whole book about it one day! It's one of the most delightful, desirable things a human can experience.

The reason I talk about playing tennis so often is because it's where I have most often been *in the zone*. Sometimes I maintain the *flow state* for several weeks. In that state, I win every match, even if the opponent is normally better than me. If my momentum breaks, it can take weeks before I get back into flow. Because I am a coach of optimal performance, I closely observe the factors causing flow and falling out of flow.

There are levels of flow, from simply lucid and "things working out to my favor" to supernatural. That's when the ball looks as big as a beach ball and floats toward me in slow motion, as if I had all day to position the racket. Someone just hit a serve into the far corner at 70 mph. My jumping there and scooping it up would be next to impossible without the flow-state. My skill certainly isn't at that level yet. I am able to ***whip*** the ball where ever I like with incredible ***velocity*** and ***precision***. But this magical level is rare. It might be too windy, too hot or I might be playing with someone who has a bad vibe. But those are excuses. Were I to intend flow more deeply, I could also get into it in bad circumstances.

At the highest level of flow, I'm not even trying. It's a blast. "He/She makes it look so easy" is what they'll say about you. An athlete's reflex actions, the position of their body and their tools (in my case a tennis racket), one's focus and **timing** (judgment of time, space and velocity) are all inner, mental and emotional processes. That's why success in sports is not only a matter of physical training but also mental and emotional training.

Flowy Golf players who get a hole in one have reported that it felt like the ball traveled on a straight, pre-determined laser-beam and the hole seemed gigantic. Flowy Quarterbacks have said that time slowed to a point where it seemed they had all day to find someone to pass the ball to and their pass was like a magnet to the receiver. Flowy Soccer players have reported feeling in this state, like shooting a goal is unavoidable and can often predict that it will happen within minutes (and it does).

So how do I get into this state????????

If only I had an answer that always works! I wish I knew! But there are a few behaviors that prepare the ground. I will explain them using tennis as an example, but they apply to all other areas (beyond sports):

1. **Soft Focus.** Rigid Attention is the greatest block to flow. Attention becomes rigid when we feel under pressure through our own expectations, the opponent's superiority, unresolved emotional issues, etc. Focus becomes too hard and I stare at the ball, the opponent or elsewhere. In this case, I need to slow down. It sounds paradoxical that slowing down would increase my performance, but that's exactly what happens. If I **s l o w** down, the ball **s l o w s** down. A trick I *often* use is to hit the ball slightly later than I normally would. This puts me into an **e x p a n d e d** mental state because it assumes I have more time to hit the ball. Even if I do not get to a state of magic, it puts me in control of myself and the game. I just wait about 1 second longer. Yes, this

applies to other things too: On your next phone call, why not wait 3-5 seconds longer before responding? Your answer will be more to your liking, because it will be more conscious. Another way to soften attention is to stop looking in the same way. I'll begin noticing the clouds, the surroundings, the trees, the hills, the birds, the players on other courts. This opening of attention softens attention. When attention is fixated, there is a drop in awareness. The flow state is high awareness (but without effort). Soft Focus is neither a loss of focus nor over-focus.

2. **Let go of worry.** Typical concerns are about winning or losing. What others think of you. What you think of others. That it's too hot or cold. The way to let go of these during play is to acknowledge they are there and intend to release them on the out-breathe. Simple as that. Unless something is a big issue for you, then you require an Emotional Releasing session. You might think that "wanting to win" is a good thing, but it won't help you with Flow. Have you ever noticed how you play much better when you no longer care whether you win or lose but play for the sake of enjoyment? Yes, intend to win, but that's different from wanting to win or worrying about it. It's a brief intention at the start of a match or phase.

3. **Fully Embrace the Situation As-Is.** Letting go of mental resistance supports flow. As long as you are not 100% committed and present, you won't experience flow. If you are wishing or thinking of being elsewhere, doing something else, or if you are distracted, you won't be present. Eagerly, being "into it" will create flow. This is a different state than being a dissociated observer. The dissociated observer state is also useful, but not for flow. In flow, you are not the observer, but fully identified with what is going on. Reality gets an effortless, liquid quality, because there is no observer-self monitoring the situation. It's as if you are slightly drunk, with a mind deeply at ease, but without the unconsciousness or unawareness of drunkenness. One could say it's a meta-observer, not a critical-observer that's present. The meta-observer is aware of what is happening, but has no preference or label on it.

Soft Worry-less Focus and Presence support the state of Flow. Having an opponent similar to your own level also helps. If the opponent is much worse or much better, no back-and-forth momentum can be developed.

I've been able to transfer the state to business, family and elsewhere. Just the other day, I told someone to buy certain stocks. He did. He made thousands of dollars within a few days. What he doesn't know: I know nothing about that stock. Then why did I tell him to get it? Intuition. Intuition comes from flow. It's inexplicable. Magic. In flow, you often know things, but don't know why you know them. It's a no-mind state. I have a long history of accurate predictions. But if you press me to explain how I knew these things, I couldn't tell you why. Intuition doesn't follow the rules. "Fred, you are not supposed to do it that way!" I have often heard, in different contexts. But I do it anyway, and it works. Why didn't I get those stocks? I'm not into stocks, I find it boring. Following things you enjoy (rather than things that bore you), supports the state of Flow.

How to be in a better flow with your Partner, spouse, Friend: Be present without expectation. Present, label-less attention is the greatest gift you can give a person. And if you could just put your phone aside for some time and put your own opinions and automatic-responses and beliefs and prejudices aside for some time and just be open to... whatever!... you can get into a flow state with your partner and surprising things can happen.

When on vacation, is it better to plan or to "go with the flow"? My definitive answer to this is: If you cannot get into flow, it's *much better* to Plan. But if you are practiced in higher states of consciousness, it's better to be without a plan. My solution? I choose the effortless, intention-less, definition-less no-plan vacation. But just in case I don't get into flow, I have a backup-plan. I do the same for seminars. My seminars are done spontaneously. But I have a backup plan just in case.

Can the magic of flow be used in gambling? Yes it can, and no, I don't. In Basketball there is a term called "hot ball". That's when a team has momentum and every ball seems to go in. In Casinos, there is a term called "cooler". That's someone who comes in and disturbs the energy just in case a person is in a too good of a flow. The trick to using flow in gambling is to quit the first time you are out of flow. Don't be tempted to continue. You might be in flow and make several wins. But if you make one loss, quit. Then you still have a plus. However, I don't gamble. Why not? Because there are so many better ways to use flow. Casinos and online betting is always rigged against you and the scene is full of seedy and desperate characters. The Get-rich-quick-mentality often found here is poverty-thinking.

Negative people and events disrupt flow. Honesty supports flow. Suppression disrupts flow. Free communication supports flow. The most common flow disruption comes from being too ambitious. Over-focused people never enjoy the stuff they work so hard to achieve. Nor do they ever achieve anything without hard work. In flow, work is much easier. If you hope to attain flow, you neither under-perform nor over-perform. You hit the sweet-spot in the middle.

3

The Space In Which
Thoughts Arise

A Meditation for a lighter state of consciousness. Leave between 15 and 120 seconds for each item.

You think thoughts are important?

You'd like to share your thoughts?

You'd like to know my thoughts?

There is something more important than thoughts: the space in which thoughts arise. And who thoughts arise to.

Softly put attention on thought or become aware of your stream of thought. Keep it there for a minute.

Thoughts arise and fade away like waves in the ocean. They come and go.

While putting attention on thought, can you also be aware of the space and silence in which thought arises?

You've spent a lifetime reading and listening to people's thoughts, opinions, ideas, beliefs. And your own. But what about the space that contains them?

Every thought begins and ends, starts and fades, arises and decays. Could you become aware of the space and silence before and after a thought? Could you keep awareness of that for a minute or more?

Could you be aware of the space and silence around thoughts as well as the space and silence permeating thoughts?

While softly putting attention on thoughts, could you, at the same time, become aware of *where*, in the body, thoughts arise? Does thought appear to arise from the foot, the knees, the hips, the stomach, the chest, the throat, the forehead, or elsewhere?

Yes, if you take the time to look, you'll find that thoughts typically arise from locations in the body or your energy field.

While softly putting attention on thoughts, could you, at the same time, become aware of *where* thoughts fade away?

Could you put awareness on where thoughts arise and where they fade away, and the silence and space before and after thought?

Could you now become aware of *who* all these thoughts occur to? *Who* is having these thoughts? What is this sense of self for *who* thoughts arise?

And could you, at the same time, be aware of the silence and space surrounding this sense of self?

Could you repeat this meditation a few times until it becomes normal to not only be aware of thoughts but of the space and silence they arise in?

An audio-version of this meditation can be downloaded in the "Members" section of my website.

4

Don't Try So Hard, Let Your Subconscious Do It For You

There are two ways to achieve something. One: Sheer willpower, practice and concentration. Two: Effortless intent and letting go. You visualize the desired outcome and then let go to let your subconscious or "the Universe" take care of the rest. Both ways are legit, but the second way is rarely trusted, even though it can achieve greater results.

Today I'd like to give you a direct experience of the power of the second way. For this experiment, you will need a target to shoot at, and a ball or projectile. A bow and arrow. Or a bottle and a ball. A golf club and a hole. A tennis racket, a ball and a bottle. A soccer ball and a goal. All sports have the deeper purpose of learning about these two types of manifesting.

Method 1: Take 10 shots at your target from a distance that makes success moderately difficult. Do it with the "trying hard" method. Using concentration, repetition and will, try everything in your power to hit the target. Note how many times you hit the target. If you did not hit the target at all, note how close you got.

Method 2: Now take around 30 seconds to relax, breathe and **visualize** hitting the target. Imagine the motion of throwing or shooting and then hitting it at the center. Then, let go and take 10 shots at the target. Don't "try to hit the target", just trust your body, allowing it to throw or shoot in that general direction, without monitoring or controlling. If you miss the target, do not worry. Continue to trust that your body knows better and will dutifully follow what you visualized. Note how many times you hit the target. If you did not hit the target, note how close you got.

Repeat this exercise in different ways, perhaps with different tools over a few days, so that you learn the difference between the two modes. I mean it: **repeat this exercise!** Your life could depend on it! Wouldn't you love to learn a more effective way of being?

There is nothing wrong with the first way. Concentration, willpower and practice help you eventually achieve the goal. After some time, you'll be able to hit the target more often. If something does not manifest with the second way, resort to the first way.

But the second way is magical. It requires less effort at greater result. **Most people who conduct the experiment are surprised that their body "somehow knows" how to move to hit the target.** They get more hits than with the first method.

Have you ever visualized body movements or sports while falling asleep and wondered why your arm or leg suddenly jerk on their own? They follow the orders of what you imagine. All of creation follows the orders of consciousness.

The challenge is in letting go/trusting. Normally, if there is a miss or failure, the mind goes back to relying on itself and it's concentrating, willpowering, efforting, gripping ways. I highly recommend you continue trusting, even if there are mistakes. You visualized it and your body has learned and will start adjusting. If you can deepen the trust, your body will do things you thought are impossible.

Fortunately, visualizing outcomes and letting go not only applies to the body, but to life.

Most people have this state when they do something for the first time. If they are relaxed about it, it flows effortlessly. Later, as they accumulate too many assumptions about it, they lose natural ease and the intervening mind takes over. This intervening, controlling part of the self is the fearful self.

The second way does not lack interest. It's an attention different from concentration. More of a **relaxed awareness**. But not so relaxed, that it's dull. It's a trust that comes from the heart.

5

Without Losing,
There Is No Winning

"What if I don't make it as a singer? I'd feel like a loser. Maybe I should pursue something more realistic," a student recently told me. The word "loser" stuck out at me. Losing is one thing, defining oneself as "a loser" a whole other. With a sense of compassion, I responded:

"A loser is not someone who loses a challenge, it is someone who doesn't even try, out of fear of losing."

I lose a lot. That's a good sign. It means I don't shy away, I participate. **Not participating in life because you fear losing is much worse than losing.**

I enter a sports match against players much better than I. Even though I know I will probably lose. Why? Why not just avoid the humiliation? **Because I can learn the most against opponents who are better than I.** Only the insecure require everything to be "safe and easy"—all that cozy comfort won't help you grow. There is much to learn in losing and "not making it".

Sometimes I take on projects that might overwhelm me at first. Or I enter projects that might not make me much money. I don't mind "losing", because of this:

Any inventor failed a thousand times before they had a breakthrough.

Any baseball player had a thousand misses before they hit a home run.

Any money investor can tell of hundreds of misses before they learned how the market works.

But if you're afraid of losing, you won't allow yourself to fail even once. And then you can never learn the game. So you can never succeed at it. So it is true that…

Losing is a part of success!

I win some, I lose some, but I keep playing. Even if I lose, I learn and grow. I get stronger. If I hadn't played to begin with, there is no growing.

If my student pursues a singing career, she will either make it a singer, which is a win, or she won't. Then she will learn. Which is also a win. **Either way, she wins.**

It's not win or lose, it's win or learn.

With this philosophy, you leave no space or possibility for failure. Instead of discouraging competition because you are afraid of there being a "loser", you realize that every experience is of value. Success is not an event, it's a process that contains many "wins" and "losses". But success can only happen by entering games, projects, tasks, contexts, realities. So do not avoid challenges, social encounters, new tasks, new jobs and a couple of risks. Be **eager to play.**

6

Bringers of the Dawn

I first read the book *Bringers of the Dawn* by Barbara Marciniak in 1993, when I was 19 years old. As every couple of years, I was packing boxes of books for giving away and I came across the old book. I flipped through it, reading a few lines. I wasn't expecting much, having all but forgotten what the book was about. I was surprised at how current or timeless it sounded. It might as well have been written this year. These are the passage I read:

The ultimate tyranny in a society is not control by martial law. It is control by the psychological manipulation of consciousness, through which reality is defined so that those who exist within it do not even realize that they are in prison. They do not even realize that there is something outside of where they exist. We represent what is outside of what you have been taught exists. It is where you sometimes venture and where we want you to dwell; it is outside of where society has told you you can live.

You have been controlled like sheep in a pen by those who think they own you—from the government to the World Management Team to those in space. You have been deprived of knowledge by frequency control. Think of frequency as individual broadcasting and receiving through which you dial into the station of your choice. It is the broadcasting of carrier waves of intelligence. The range of frequency is unlimited, and the range of intelligent matter transmitted is unlimited.

Frequency control limits the number of stations you can tune into. As members of the Family of Light, you must anchor new frequencies through static chaos and bring them into the physical realm. The range of accessibility on this planet to a variety of frequencies has been very minimal for a long time because of many things that you most desperately need to become aware of. As you learn about your own personal history and discover patterns of ineffectual behavior that you must break and change, the planet pulses through its own patterns of behavior. You are about to repeat history as a planet in a most dramatic way.

You have come to alter and remove the frequency of limitation and to bring in the frequency of information. When you are informed, you move beyond the need to be in fear. When you feel uninformed and out of control, you do not understand the bigger picture. Each of you came to awaken something inside yourself, inside the coding of your being—the DNA—and you are responding to it. This is why you are on a search in all directions of your life.

You and multitudes of others have begun the mutation process on the planet. As you mutate electromagnetically, you alter your frequency or the tune that you broadcast. You will eventually outgrow the frequency that holds you down and continually blasts you with chaos and confusion. Eventually, when you alter, carry, and maintain your own frequency, you will vibrate differently and thus affect everyone around you. They will feel the availability of this frequency alteration, which will then move like a wave around the planet. As the planet accepts this new frequency that you have worked very hard to obtain, those at the end of the domino chain will receive it. This new frequency is called knowledge, light, and information. It is called being taken out of bondage. You are being taken out of disinformation and misinformation and you are becoming informed; you are coming into light.

As each of you has been assigned to become informed and to bring about a frequency alteration on this planet, you must learn to become Keepers of Frequency. You must rise to a certain place of knowledge and consistently stay there. You must become in command of your body so that you can will it into stillness or into activity. You must be able to go inside yourself and heal what needs to be healed emotionally and physically. You must begin to part the jungle of self and find the clearing so that you can show others the way. Sometimes you will show others rated, and they focus on what they do not have in common or label themselves different from others, it is a perfect disguise to keep them from discovering what they do have in common. This separation keeps people from banding together and becoming very strong.

Much of the political maneuvering going on, particularly in the United States, is purposely designed to separate you. Look at the New Age. Do you see how the New Age is separated? All kinds of things are said to keep you from discovering what you have in common. When people discover this, they will begin to get angry. As more and more of the methods of control and separation are revealed to you, the anger will build in the United States. Events will occur that may look as if the country is falling apart, yet they will serve the purpose of bringing people together. A new pride and a new sense of integrity will come about, because this is what is designed for the times.

I couldn't agree more.

The "game" is to keep us separated and in a low frequency. Winning the game is to first raise our own frequency and then unify with others in the pursuit of the good, true, and abundant. And even though 2020 seemed like things were falling apart, **people have really become more interested, awake and unified.** They are asking all the right questions about health, Government, freedom, community, Civil Rights, etc. But it took a crisis to awaken from complacent comfort.

The book is *vintage reality creation*, and I decided not to give it away just yet.

7

How Reality Creation Was Used
To Escape Imprisonment

I was browsing through the 1990 book Escape from Controlled Custody, from my Library of Survivalist Books. One chapter features ways prison inmates have escaped from confinement. I discovered that *most* of successful escapes use the method of **Acting-As-If,** which is an essential Reality Creation tools.

Even more interesting: The acting-as-if method is used by prisoners of war (soldiers and officers), less by common criminals. Criminals use more simple (but less successful) methods, such as tunnel digging. POWs use the more successful role-playing. That says something about the difference in consciousness levels!

From the book:

The White Line in the Road

Two Allied soldiers escaped from their camp using a bucket of white paint and two brushes. They began by painting a white line down the center of the road that led through the main gate. When they arrived at the camp exit, they lit cigarettes and appeared to be goofing off. A guard told them to keep on working, and opened the inner gate so that they could get on with the job. When they reached the outer gate, another guard opened it to allow them to continue painting the line. They continued to paint the line until they were out of sight, and then took off.[1]

The Workman

In WWI, a certain Lieutenant Marcus Kaye of the Royal Flying Corps hid articles of civilian clothing, and a bag of metal scraps intended to simulate tools, inside the latrine. Just before shift change, he went into the latrine and changed his clothing, coming out dressed as a civilian and with his face and hands smeared with dirt, as a civilian laborer might look. He dismantled and inspected part of latrine's ventilation duct. When he had that section of it reassembled, he nodded to the guard to indicate that he had to climb the ladder to inspect the top section too. He then climbed the ladder out of the prison, inspected the pipe, and made his way down the hill to freedom.

Impersonating a Ferret

The roving inspectors known as "ferrets" were nuisances, but in one camp they inadvertently provided a means of escape. At Stalag Luft III, an RAF officer who spoke perfect German observed that, when the ferrets came in to inspect the camp at night, they unlocked the inner gate themselves, and identified themselves to the tower guards by shining their flashlights on the ground as they walked. They would then inspect where they wished, or go spend an hour in the kitchen. This behavior pattern suggested a way out.

The officer improvised a ferret uniform, which was only a jumpsuit, belt, and field service type cap. He also arranged for a POW with locksmithing skill to produce a master key to open the gate's padlock. He also obtained a flashlight by bribing a guard. He arranged for false papers, allowing him to travel inside Germany, and settled down to wait for the right moment.

One night, when the ferret was inside the compound, the escaper slipped out of his window and walked towards the inner gate, shining his flashlight upon the ground. He opened the gate with his key, but was unable to lock the padlock. He pushed it almost closed, and went towards the outer gate, where his false papers got him past the guard. He was several miles away from the camp when the genuine ferret

I have a few stories of my own. Many years ago, I was contacted by a South Korean who wanted me to help her sister escape North Korea. She had some way of getting messages to her sister, but naturally wouldn't share them with me. I instructed the sister to go through the entire successful escape from start to finish, in every detail and every day, for months—backwards. She was to start by imagining hugging her sister and then work back from there: What happened before that? And before that? And how did you get to that point? And what happened before that? She was priming her subconscious and body-memory to a successful escape.

The most crucial part of the escape was a river in the wilderness. It was freezing. Most who attempted to escape on that route, in the winter, died. But if one could survive it, escape was fairly straightforward. That's why visualizing warmth and comfort during the crossing of the river was the most important part of the daily visualization. Every day, she went through a meditation routine where she saw herself going the whole journey. I cannot share more details of the story, except to say that it was successful and also involved elaborate role-playing after she had reached China. We had forgotten to add any visualization for the trip from China to South Korea and it proved almost ass difficult as escaping North Korea. In the end, she achieved her goal and is now safe and happy with her sister, the last I heard.

Whether we can leave or enter a place is not only determined by external factors. It also depends on our inner state.

When I was 17 and 18, I used to get into dance clubs by saying to the doorkeeper, "They are with me", pointing to my friends standing behind me. This implied that the doorkeeper was somehow supposed to know who I am and that my VIP-status entitled me to get other people into the club. 9 times out of 10, this trick worked. If I didn't use the trick, we'd often be rejected at the door. Only once, it did not work, and the gatekeeper boomed "And who the fuck are YOU?". It was an embarrassing moment. All the other times, it worked because only a VIP would talk that way and the doorman and they wouldn't dare question it.

Once, I entered a country on an expired visa. It had expired months ago, but neither the airport check-in, nor the immigration officers, noticed. What helped was that I *didn't know* it had expired. I only discovered that while flipping through my passport on the way to the Hotel. Because I assumed that all was well, I felt well and so all went well.

This article is not to imply that you should embark upon a career as a con-artist. It is to say that, if you ever find yourself in a critical situation, it is important to maintain a good, calm, joyful inner state. Even if you had a gun pointed at you, you should not give in to fear. Keep attention on a more pleasant scenario. This could save your life. It is impossible for you to feel good, at a fundamental level, and experience something bad.

If you ever find yourself in a crucial situation, learn to maintain a good state. Even if you have a gun pointed at you, do not give in to fear and keep your attention on a more pleasant scenario. It is impossible for you to feel something good and experience something bad. But if you succumb to fear, a bad experience becomes possible.

8

A Time for Civil Disobedience

Worldwide death rates have stayed much the same for 2018, 2019, 2020 and 2021. That's a **fact** anyone can look up. Whether people die from the common flu, cancer, car accidents or from COVID, the fatality rate remains the same. Death is an unavoidable fact of life and no amount of legislation, lockdown or vaccine has changed that. If your time has come to pass on to the next life, even wearing three sanitized masks won't change that. The *organizing principle of creation* (you call it Nature, Universe or God) has a plan for a pre-determined amount of births and deaths. Some have written that the moment of your death was determined before you were even born.

In places without lockdown, death rates were no higher or lower in percentage than in places with lockdown. That too is a **fact** that you can look up.

Tyrants in History, have always liked the idea of "the greater good" to justify their oppression. In 2020 and 2021, I have coached many good people who were forced out of business "for the greater good". It's not their neighbors who have asked them to stop running their business, it's "the Government", whatever that is. Within the year, I have worked with:

a gym owner,

a restaurant owner,

the owner of a tourist activities company,

an owner of Hotels,

a traveling photographer

And a few others. These people come from different countries–USA, Germany, Switzerland, Australia and Morocco. You'd think they are *different* countries, but they all appear to follow the same failed collectivist politics. In each case, the State forced them to shut down their business. If they didn't, they were either penalized or arrested. Then they were coerced into taking loans from the Government and to be in their debt. Using the words **"forced" and "coerced"** here is entirely appropriate. Businesses and countless families that depend on them have been destroyed. All for "the greater good". People being forced to take loans from a specific source is no different from a mafia shakedown. And this is what we call "the Government"?

These Businesses and families are the backbone of our society. Strategists are dazzled: Entire nations have been subdued without a single shot being fired!

When they come to me for Coaching, what am I supposed to tell them? Reality Creation Coaching *assumes* that it is allowed for a person to offer products or services they like, in exchange for money. When the time comes where that is no longer allowed, I will discard *Reality Creation Coaching* and teach civil disobedience instead.

I know, there are many who *demand* lockdowns and restrictions. I respect that. They are scared. Maybe you are among those who demand lockdowns. If so, please consider this: Fear attracts the things you are afraid of. Have no fear and you become immune to illness. You might say "We should have lockdowns because the majority wants lockdowns". But that's not how a free society works. The will of the majority should not erase the civil rights of a minority. Even if you disagree with my stance on COVID, the shift of Governments worldwide toward overt dictatorship should worry you. Rules are implemented without examination, discussion or votes. The views of a large part of trained medical doctors are ignored. People are snitching on their neighbors. In many countries, freedom of travel, movement, association and speech are suspended–with no vote being counted!

Should the interests of the individual be suppressed for "the greater good"? No. **A Government that uses the "greater good" concept has failed arrange things between different parties**, has failed to respect the rights of one group of people in favour of another. A Government that sacrifices the prosperity of Millions for the hypothetical health of a dozen, has utterly failed, or has a hidden agenda.

Even if you disagree with me on Covid-19, don't you think Government measures should have been openly discussed?

Who defines "greater good"? For who is it good? Covid, so far, has been very good for the wealth of Amazon, Apple, Facebook, Netflix, Google and Microsoft. **Covid has been the greatest wealth transfer from middle to upper class in History**. It hasn't been good for the middle class.

And what do lockdowns keep us safe from? From social interaction? From living independent of Government handouts? Does it keep a child safe to no longer have friends and instead stare at screens all day? The social, psychological and physical consequences of lockdowns are *much worse* than having flu symptoms for a week.

I see some colleagues of mine, saying that lockdowns should be "embraced" and we should think positively about them. I'm all for making the best of a situation. But should they really be embraced, or should they be defied?

If we were talking about an actual pandemic—you know, the kind that fills hospitals, then nobody would be talking civil disobedience. But hospitals stand empty. Remember when you were told that lockdowns would solve the issue? And it didn't? Remember when you were told that vaccines would solve the issue? And now they are saying they don't, because there are "mutations" of the virus and you'll have to stay out of Business indefinitely?

And remember when thousands of restaurants across Italy, defied Government orders to close? That was coordinated and **peaceful civil disobedience**. Or maybe you don't remember it, because you didn't hear about it. And maybe you didn't hear about it because you only read mainstream news. And maybe that's evidence that mainstream news is state-sponsored propaganda. Many Italians kept their restaurants open and there was nothing "the Government" could do about it, because we-the-people are the real Government. We outnumber public officials by about 700 000. **YOU are the Government!** For every public official, there are 700 000 people. It is our own will that determines our reality. If enough people keep their Businesses open, there is nothing they can do about it.

Or can they? Well, they could behave like the CCP and send in police to haul people off to prison. But if they did that, it would reveal that they are not on our side, which would eventually cause an even greater uprising. So that's unlikely to happen. But to make sure that never happens, more people need to practice peaceful civil disobedience.

You may think that the act of one person has no influence at all, but it does. Your influence is accumulative.

"If a law is unjust, a man is not only right to disobey it, he is obligated to do so."

Thomas Jefferson

9

Happy-Go-Lucky Investment

Around the beginning of January, I acquired a large amount of Bitcoin. Half a year ago, I also acquired a good amount of silver. It was the first time in my life that I bought either. There was no specific reason for it. Then, in February 2021, both silver and bitcoin shot up in value, giving me significant earnings.

A friend of mine, who has been obsessing over investments for decades, said to me: *"You know your stuff, don't you. You know more than you let on"*. In reality, I know next to *nothing* about the market. I don't even know why my bitcoin is suddenly worth tens of thousands of Dollars more. I assume it's because Elon Musk said that his company would accept Bitcoin? Fine. But really, I don't know a thing about Bitcoin, Silver, or the the stock market. I do not read Investment Blogs, do not follow investment trends.

"What's your approach, Fred?", "What's your method, Fred?". Well, I don't think anyone should follow my investment advice, because I am:

Happy-Go-Lucky

Happy-Go-Lucky people succeed naively. They don't have a plan, a strategy or any attachment. We do not obsess over money. Money is an Illusion. Bitcoin is even more of an Illusion. It only has reality because people believe it does. Bitcoin doesn't even exist as a tangible value. Silver is less of an Illusion, but the value ascribed to it, is. Silver is stuff dug up from the ground and then labeled as "valuable". The same with the US Dollar. It has value because people say it does. But really, it's just paper that symbolizes value. Bitcoin is just numbers on a screen. Silver is just a clunk of stuff dug up from the ground. Real Estate? Now that's real value. That's why it's called **REAL** Estate.

◀)) # happy-go-lucky
/ ˌhapɪɡəʊˈlʌki/

adjective

cheerfully unconcerned about the future.
"a happy-go-lucky attitude"

Similar: easy-going   carefree   casual   free and easy

My friend, who obsesses over money, told me I need to sell my Bitcoin now, because it's at its height. But I'm not. Whether it goes up or down in value, doesn't bother me. If it goes down, oh well. If it goes up, fine. All this stress people have over money, is ridiculous. I don't see my bitcoin, US-Dollars or silver as real assets. My real assets are my books.

The point of this article: Don't be scared. Your true assets are **inside you**. They cannot be taken away from you. EVER. You can generate abundance over and over, at any time, any place. Knowing that, is being truly rich. Winning or losing money "in the market" is irrelevant.

"Oh, all that new agey talk sounds nice Fred, but my investments feed my family!".

Chill out. Your investments don't feed your family. If anything, it's your intuitive talent for investing, that feeds your family. And if you have that intuitive talent today, you can still have it in 10 years. And then you'll always be on the safe side, financially. It's all INSIDE. That's not new agey talk. Don't you trust you can provide for yourself and others? If not, isn't that the first problem? Doesn't that problem need to get fixed first, before we talk about investing?

I say it's the first thing to fix: Your feeling that you are creative, smart and capable of creating and generating abundance now and in the future. If you have that, you stop worrying and all else false into place.

The term happy-go-lucky is a real word in the English language. And it reveals something interesting about life: People who are happy… they go lucky! That means, there is no such thing as "luck" for no reason. To be lucky, you first have to be in a higher energy, you have to be happy. Happy goes Lucky. And indeed, I know a few languages in which the words "Happiness" and "Luck" are the same word! No difference! People I have taught languages to in the past were confused: How do I know it's "Luck" vs. "Happiness" if it's the same word? is what they'd ask me. And now I say: You don't, because they are the same.

10

Identity Shifting, Multiple Personality Disorder or Possession?

A friend was recounting a story about his grandmother changing personality at times. In one identity she was frail and weak, barely able to walk. In the other identity she was able to carry two heavy gas canisters on each shoulder.

In response, I relayed a story of how I used to play soccer with a group of seniors, aged 60 to 90 (!). Some of them had difficulty walking. Some held on to rails. But when they were on the playing field, it was as if they had changed identity. They ran quick as rabbits. When it came to scoring, their limp mysteriously vanished.

In my 2006 book Parallel Universes of Self, I ascribe reality shifts to changes in *Identity*. If you can shift self-image, you shift what you experience. I also wrote about Multiple Personality Disorder and how patients radically change, depending on which Identity they are occupying.

My friend telling me about his grandmother, triggered another, less pleasant memory of my grandmother changing her personality. It was a forgotten memory until that moment. How could I have forgotten? I hadn't even remembered while writing "Parallel Universes of Self". How expert we are at repressing unattractive truths!

As a child I sometimes stayed overnight at my grandmothers. I enjoyed that. But at sometimes, her personality changed. There was a side she never showed on family visits in the daytime. In those strange hours, there was a different presence permeating the house, and it terrified me. When she went into this persona, she quit talking or showing any interest in me. Looking at her face I saw "my grandmother" was no longer there. How unsettling! It felt like a man had entered her body and not just any man, but one filled with silent rage. When it happened, I'd usually retreat to the bedroom and pretend to be sleeping. "Grandmother" would then engage in uncharacteristic activities. Instead of sitting in her reclining chair watching TV or reading a book, she'd wander around the house and rummage through shelves and closets, as if looking for something.

What is going on here? Just a child's imagination run wild? I don't think so. The presence was alien, nothing like my grandmother. When the presence arrived, I could feel it before I even saw her. She might be in another room and I knew she was no longer herself before she entered the room I was in. She wouldn't say a word, wouldn't smile, wouldn't interact. In her normal state, she talked to me at length about History, World Events and the Family. But under the weird spell, she ceased all communication and wouldn't even tuck me in or say goodnight.

Insight: Both entity possession and identity shifting, as I teach it in my coaching, give you a new personality and new skills. Either can provide superhuman strength or unusual ability. In fact, one day before writing this article, I had to use the technique. I was kayaking out in the open ocean, but the weather had changed. The waters had become difficult to navigate. As I am not experienced in kayaking, I felt unsettled. To quell my fears and make it out of the waters alive, I had to shift my identity. I imagined myself to be an experienced man of the sea, who had spent his entire lifetime in kayaks and boats. The identity shift helped me find the calm to return to safety.

And that's the difference between *identity-shifting* and *multiple personality disorder* or *entity possession*. Identity-Shifting is deliberate. It's consciously chosen.

I have walked over hot coals without burning my feet or getting blisters. That was at a Tony Robbins Seminar I attended more than a quarter century ago (how time flies!). I achieved the state by imagining I am made of Ice and the hot coals are made of ice. I stomped my feet to the music, imagining the ice for twenty minutes, before venturing on to the hot coals.

But I've also seen a woman *eat* hot coal, without getting any burns or blisters on her face. This was at a festival in North Africa. But the situation was much less inspiring than me walking over hot coal. She was not being herself and was not eating the hot coal voluntarily and everyone could tell. People were appalled. Her eyes kept rolling out of her eye sockets and she made horrific gurgling noises. That's entity possession.

Is it in fact entity possession or MPD? Is there a difference? I don't know. Those are just two different labels to describe a very real phenomenon. One is a spiritual label, the other is a medical label.

What I do know is that a shift in Identity creates remarkable changes. Those blind can see, those poor become rich, those fearful become fearless. But consciously choosing a new identity, vs. having a foreign id-entity take over are on two opposite ends of the spectrum of empowerment.

11

Human Made Flying Saucers

I've seen flying saucers at different times. Once I witnessed three at the same time. They were performing the moves one can only perform with saucer-shaped vehicles, such as abrupt up-down and left-right. The event *scared* me. It made me think "aliens" because I had been conditioned to think "aliens" by what I saw on TV. If you don't know what you don't know, you don't look for it. The event set me off reading about these strange aircraft for the rest of my life. Today I realize the truth about flying saucers is concealed beneath three neatly crafted layers of disinformation.

Layer 1: "Flying Saucers are Aliens,"

Layer 2: "Flying Saucers are Recent,"

Layer 3: "Nazi Flying Saucers."

Because human beings have strong intuition and can smell when something is fishy, the truth has to be hidden under several layers of falsehood and even then, it eventually surfaces.

During research for my book Extraterrestrial Linguistics, I discovered something extraordinary: The CIA (a rogue branch of the U.S. Government), secretly funded and promoted books on aliens, UFOs and Flying Saucers from the 1950s onwards. I documented this amazing fact in a short chapter in the book. Blinders fell off my eyes instantly. If they were promoting flying saucers as "Alien", then probably because they weren't! But why would they promote the idea? My guess: So that they can keep the technology in the hands of a select few.

Another lie uncovered was that flying saucers are a recent phenomenon, rather than flown and witnessed for *thousands of years*. I've also documented and proven this in the book. This article is not included in the book, it's a spin-off from it.

Between the 1920s and 1950s, there were *humans* from different countries, designing, manufacturing, and piloting flying saucers. Then, in the 50s and 60s, the "public narrative" and "image" of flying saucers changed from human-made vehicles to "alien" vehicles. To assert the new, **socially engineered narrative**, it was heavily promoted in an endless stream of Hollywood movies and hundreds of books.

Don't get me wrong, I know aliens exist. I have encountered alien life-forms (see my book "The Pleiades and Our Secret Destiny"). The Universe is teeming with intelligent life-forms. But why wouldn't any of the flying discs many of us have witnessed be human made? Human Beings are *capable* of great things. I write this article to break the conditioning that automatically links the flying discs with aliens.

Then, if anyone ever tries to pull a fake alien-invasion on you, you'll use discernment.

Rene Couzinet's Flying Saucers

The images above and below are flying saucers by French airplane engineer Rene Couzinet, who also created many conventional aircraft. Named *Couzinet RC-360*, it was a vertical-takeoff aircraft that used two counter-rotating discs that were powered by three engines. Another model was designed with six engines by the firm Lycoming and a "Viper turbojet" by Marcel Dassault. His first flying saucer was completed in Paris in 1956. Soon after, Couzinet survived a car bomb explosion (miraculously without injuries). A little later, he abruptly "commit suicide", due to "lack of success" according to Wikipedia. But I don't believe that. He was successful with regular airplanes and happily married. To friends, he sounded upbeat. Several successful test flights of his saucer had been completed and he believed they had "surpassed conventional flight techniques". Why would he abruptly commit suicide? Isn't it more plausible that the same people who planted a bomb in his car finally managed to kill him and make it look like suicide?

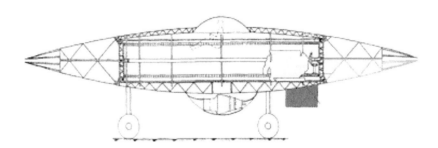

But by would there be people willing to kill for it? Because "Flying saucers" is a touchy subject. Research (presented in aforementioned book) taught me that the saucer shape has been the normal shape of interstellar aircraft for thousands of years. It's not true that they just suddenly appeared in the late 1940s, as all the "UFO Books" tell us. They were there in the 1930s, 1920s, 1910s, in the 17th, 16th, 15th Century, 1000 B.C., 5000 B.C. and further back. Technology did not just suddenly start with the industrial revolution 200 years ago.

The CIA and similar unaccountable, rogue organizations in other countries created both the myth of "alien UFOs" and also endless denials. They provided the fake, easily debunk-able photos and footage of "aliens" and they also provided the debunkers and "skeptics". *Providing both sides—the Alien-Enthusiasts and the Debunkers is the best way to manifest rumors as "truth" and obfuscate the reality of human-made discs.* You can tell that most of these "UFO Skeptics" are paid operatives by this: They make no mention of human made UFOs, nor of CIA-funding of UFO-Literature. They are paid to attack the idea of "Alien UFOs" exclusively, as *to convince more people of the opposite.* It's reverse mass-psychology. Two sides fight while a third remains hidden.

The "Flying Top" by Rudolf Schriever

This flying saucer was produced in factories in the areas of Dresden, Germany and Wroclaw, Poland by German engineers Rudolf Schriever and Otto Habermohl, Shriever test-piloted his own flying saucers.

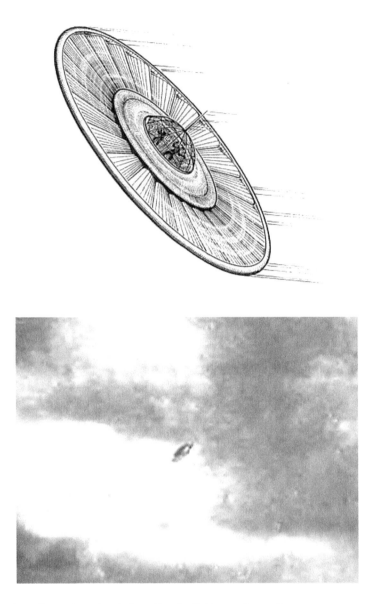

As with others involved in disc-building, there is controversy about the cause of Shrievers death at age 44. He was said to have died in a car accident on the 16th of January 1953. Others say he died due to complications after the car accident. Yet other sources say he had a heart-attack. And then there are those who say he was murdered. Yet others say that he did not die in January, but October 1953. And there are those who say he died in the 1960s. When you have this many versions of a story, you are dealing with some "agency" that is "seeding" false information. It's routine work by "intelligence" agencies to obfuscate "sensitive" truths.

Shifting Narratives

The "Gray Aliens", small, lanky beings with big black eyes and enormous, bulbous heads, only began surfacing in the 1970s and gained widespread popularity in the 1990s. Before that, most UFOs were supposedly piloted by handsome blonde haired men and sexy women. This gradual shift in narrative is the clearest sign that the whole "Alien UFOs" myth is socially engineered propaganda. In the 1950s and 1960s, the UFO-pilots were our "space brothers" come to warn us of the dangers of nuclear war. Then, in the 1970s to 1990s, they were the "Gray Aliens", abducting and experimenting on people, involving some kind of "anal probe" in 70% of reports. What about all these "anal probes" in connection with UFOs? This has been the butt of jokes for decades. But could it be that people dressed as aliens were abducting humans, drugging them, and then sexually abusing them? Who knows!

In the 1990s, commercial implant technology hit the medical market. Concurrent with that, there was an increase in "abductee reports" of the "aliens" giving people implants. UFO- and New Age Magazines were now full of such stories, but they weren't before that! As time passed and implants became smaller, the devices implanted by "Aliens" also became smaller. If we are dealing with "advanced extraterrestrial technology", why did their technology mirror human progress?

Looking just at the bare facts, what we have are flying discs in our skies, witnessed by Millions of people. What's so difficult about building a flying disc? Why does it have to be "alien"? If people weren't as forgetful as they are, they'd see how the narrative shifted from human-made saucers in the 1930s and 1940s, to space brothers in the 1950s and 1960s, to Gray Aliens in the 1970s to 1990s. And today, in 2020? The field of

"Ufology" is still full of that **intangible, vague nothingness** so typical of disinformation.

The Myth of Nazi UFOs

If you break through the disinformation layer that "flying saucers are alien", the next layer you usually reach is that they were created by Adolf Hitler and deployed by Nazis and that these Nazis still fly them and have secret bases in the Antarctic or even on the moon. If you have never heard of this idea, you haven't dug deep enough. Most people haven't even dug into the "aliens" layer, because they can't be bothered. But some dig and research until they hit upon this one.

This alternative socially engineered "narrative" is that the Nazis developed saucers they called "Vril" and "Haunebu". Some add that the construction plans for these saucers were channeled by a woman named Maria Orsic, of the "Vril Society" and that the saucers have miraculous qualities. They have anti-gravity propulsion, light speed, the capability to be invisible, etc. There are hundreds of books spreading these claims, without tangible evidence.

The naïve, having once idealized and romanticized "alien space brothers", now begin idealizing and romanticizing Nazis.

One might ask: If this fantastical Nazi weapon was so advanced and Hitler had it, why didn't he deploy it to win the war?

A deeper examination and the whole thing falls apart. The "narrative" of the "Haunebu" UFOs was created in the 1970s. No researcher has found mention of the word "Haunebu" prior to the 1970s. The alleged "blueprints" of these "Nazi UFOs" (see image below), allegedly printed in the 1940s, were made with typewriter font common in the 1970s.

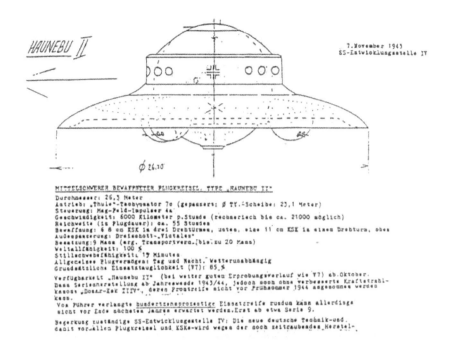

That doesn't mean there were no Germans involved in flying saucers. Plenty of Germans were building flying saucers. But these weren't necessarily "Nazis", but private inventors and airplane engineers. Most of them did not want their inventions to fall into the hands of the Government.

I have previously showcased the Austrian inventor Viktor Schauberger, who is probably the originator of the flying saucer in modern times. Schauberger manufactured implosion-based flying saucers as far back as the early 1920s, long before the Nazis appeared on the scene (image below).

Nor does it mean that the Nazis had no interest in flying saucers. They were always on the lookout for advanced aircraft that could get them an advantage in their war efforts. But it appears that the vehicles being looked into were more conventional, as in the example below.

BMWs Flying Saucers

This is a drawing of the "Flugelrad" (Flying Wheel), produced in 1938 by none other than BMW and designed by engineer Richard Miethe. BMWs interest in flying saucers is well documented, and was reported by dozens of witnesses who were involved in construction in the area of the Prague airport, formerly Prague-Ruzyne. Manufacture and Test flights were also conducted between August and September 1943 at Prague-Kbely airport.

Flying Discs ascend vertically, within seconds. They fly in angles that conventional aircraft are not capable of. There is no known case in which they were shot down by normal aircraft. Flying Saucers are superior because a spinning disc gains flight momentum of its own, at greatly reduced fuel use. This you know from throwing a Frisbee. The Frisbee can fly at some distance, *propelled by itself.* When thrown in the right way, the spinning disc can float up and down on the air over an incredible distance.

The human-made flying saucers shown in this article all use mainstream propulsion and mechanics. I am intentionally not showcasing anything out of the ordinary, such as alleged anti-gravity aircraft or discs with interstellar capabilities. My reason is to show that they could be more ordinary than the "aliens" narrative suggests.

Flying Saucers by Andreas Epp

Andreas Epp was the German inventor of several flying saucer types (as well as conventional vehicles). This is his successful "Omega Disc", completed in the 1950s:

Andreas Epp is also the inventor of a prototype Hovercraft, which he claims had been stolen from him in the 1950s by a British company. His saucers proved fully functional, but they were, according to him, ignored by industry and Government. Epp had a registered patent on his disc in Germany in 1958, called in German "fliegende Untertasse", in English "flying saucer".

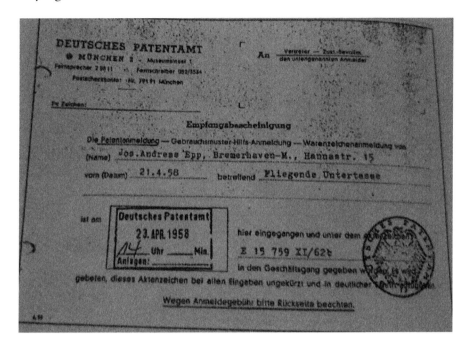

Andreas Epp claims that flying saucers were originally nothing more than improved, encased helicopters. The body of the saucer remained stable during flight or floating. The engines hung at the left and right sides of a crossbar that is also the steering bar. The pilot manually steered from the center. This is how maneuvers of up to 90 degrees are possible. Because the crossbar is connected to the cockpit, the engines are always turning when the pilot turns and always showing pointed in flight direction. Controls and fuel also run through the crossbar.

The Canadian Avro Disc

The Avro Disc, made in Canada for the U.S. Air Force, was claimed to have been a failure. But that the project existed and 10s of Millions of dollars were invested shows how seriously flying saucers were taken.

Most people aren't even aware that these projects existed. In my view, they did not fail at all. That's why they are sighted by tens of thousands of people every year. If flying saucers had "failed", we wouldn't be seeing them fly!

What usually happens when a UFO is sighted? The Government issues denials, while newspapers publish tongue-in-cheek articles about "little green men from Mars". Very rarely is anything *questioned* or followed up on.

Turboproietto

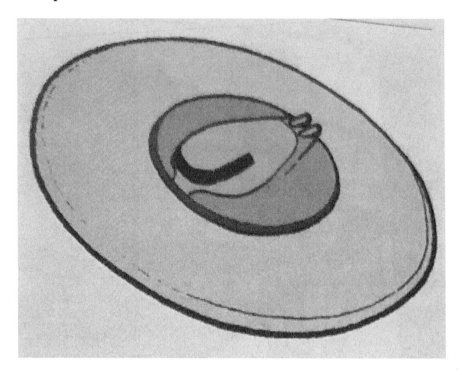

This is a drawing of the Turboproietto, a disc allegedly created by Italian Engineer G. Bellonzo. It was modeled after the example of a gyroscope or spinning top. As such, it self-stabilized. It was 10 to 15 meters in diameter. For propulsion, it possessed two ram jet engines. The outer part, with the nozzles, rotated, while the cockpit remained in a fixed position. It was said to have used an air-sucking technique that prevented the vehicle from overheating, therefore allowing higher speeds.

In those days, eye-witnesses from around Europe had come forward, saying they have seen saucers at various airports, in fields and in the air, always attended to by humans, not aliens.

Finally, here's a 1952 official CIA document, admitting to the reality of **human flying saucers.** The first major batch of books on "UFO Aliens" were published two years later, in 1954. From that point forward, the idea of "human made saucers" was eradicated from public consciousness.

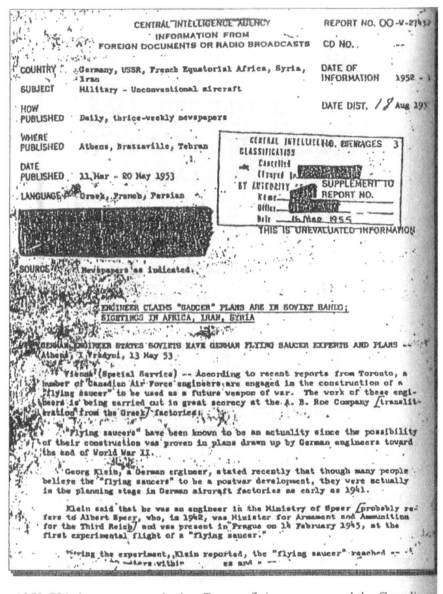

1952 CIA document mentioning German flying saucers and the Canadian AVRO saucer.

The **deeper issue** is that there are apparently shady agencies that can create mass beliefs and make people forget them again. If you have **good memory and attention span, you can't be fooled.** On our path to higher consciousness, we need to rid ourselves of organizations that create and mass-disseminate false information. Health and Abundance grow in true and reliable information.

12

The Military Is Running Parallel Earth And Mirror Earth Simulators

If you've seen the TV-Show *Westworld Season 3* (yeah, not nearly as good as Season 1), you recall a gigantic AI system, that was creating a mirror image of the world, including all people, places, things and events, even down to exact street names and terrain in order to simulate and anticipate what would happen. It could predict events for individuals, groups or even the whole world with high accuracy.

The makers of the TV-Show call this "science fiction", but it isn't. It was a reality, long before this "sci fi" show was even produced. Rather than predicting the future, it was perhaps to get people *used to* its reality in the present. There are already many variants of this AI existing today. One of them is a military-funded program called *Sentient World Simulation*. To quote (bolding mine):

The program has amassed databases so profound ***they can now look so deep into a person's life they can predict their thoughts and future actions with relative certainty.*** *Although this system is incredibly intrusive and raises many moral concerns, it provides valuable insight into questions which could be extremely beneficial. It's unclear as to whether all the private-sector* *efforts towards transparency will have any effect on the direction and intensity of public-sector surveillance.*

By gathering enough intelligence, SWS is capable of producing realistic simulations of various different scenarios such as natural disasters, foreign and domestic attacks, resource shortages, and hazardous economic trends. The program, once finished, will utilize the information from its colossal database to create these hypothetical situations, **predict possible outcomes, and test the effectiveness of various responses.** *Researchers hope the system will be able to provide effective answers to complex questions which baffle the most skilled thinkers and will create more efficient methods of responding to catastrophes.*

To read more, here is the source: Sentient World Simulation and NSA Surveillance

Pretty amazing, huh?

To anticipate how you react in real life, the programmers experiment in a virtual-reality mirror of Earth. They simulate pandemics, disasters, market crashes, hazardous weather, cut power supplies, etc. They input one scenario into the Earth-Mirror and the program spits out a few of the most likely scenarios.

The program was already being developed in 2007, as this article shows:

Sentient World Simulation (SWS)... a **"synthetic mirror of the real world with automated continuous calibration with respect to current real-world information"**

"SWS provides an environment for testing Psychological Operations (PSYOP)," the paper reads, so that military leaders can "develop and **test multiple courses of action** *to anticipate and shape behaviors of adversaries, neutrals, and partners."*

SWS also replicates financial institutions, utilities, media outlets, and street corner shops. By applying theories of economics and human psychology, its

developers believe they can predict how individuals and mobs will respond to various stressors...

(It is) now capable of running real-time simulations for up to 62 nations, including Iraq, Afghanistan, and China. **The simulations gobble up breaking news, census data, economic indicators, and climactic events in the real world, along with proprietary information such as military intelligence.**

Military and intel officials can introduce fictitious agents into the simulations (such as a spike in unemployment, for example) to gauge their destabilising effects on a population.

If this was already successfully being run in 2007 and earlier, then *Westworld Season 3* was already outdated before it was even filmed.

So... is this a good or bad thing? I don't know. I guess that depends on what kind of world you wish to live in. It's certainly an *interesting thing*. The problem right now is that only a select few people have access to this kind of data. With it, they accumulate and horde power. Will the knowledge become more widely available some day? Probably. The first people who had Internet, in the 1960s, were the U.S. Military. We got ours in the 1990s. So maybe we'll get our own private world and life simulator in another 20 years.

In my 2006 book "Parallel Universes of Self ", I say that you have many possible pasts and futures, depending on the choices you make. Would it be useful if you had a program that could show you the most likely outcomes for each choice, based on all kinds of data? Would that not make your life much easier?

I doubt it. Firstly: It would rob you of the *process* of deciding based on what you have learned and based on intuition (which is soul-knowledge that transcends space and time). Much of modern life robs you of experiencing process: You get your burger ready-made and don't experience the process of hunting, killing, skinning and cooking it. You get your clothes ready made and don't experience the process of collecting materials and weaving them. Likewise, having this computer that knows everything beforehand is the ultimate control-freak dream, but will it make people stronger, happier, and more able? Secondly: How easily could someone who owns this kind of program steer your life? Would you not become nothing more than a guinea pig in someone's gigantic reality simulation program? (Are we already in such a simulation program?)

SWS is not the only project that seeks to exercise control of reality by amassing insane amounts of data. Quoting from another article, on a project called *Sentient* (not the same as the previous one):

*Sentient is (or at least aims to be) an omnivorous analysis tool, capable of devouring data of all sorts, making sense of the past and present, anticipating the future, and **pointing satellites toward what it determines will be the most interesting parts of that future**.*

Until now, Sentient has been treated as a government secret, except for vague allusions in a few speeches and presentations. But recently released documents — many formerly classified secret or top secret — reveal new details about the program's goals, progress, and reach.

Research related to Sentient has been going on since at least October 2010…

*"It ingests high volumes of data and processes it," says Furgerson. "Sentient catalogs normal patterns, detects anomalies, and helps forecast and model adversaries' potential courses of action." The NRO did not provide examples of patterns or anomalies, but one could imagine that things like "not moving a missile" versus "moving a missile" might be on the list. Those forecasts in hand, **Sentient could turn satellites' sensors to the right place at the right time to catch ill will** (or whatever else it wants to see) in action. "Sentient is a thinking system," says Furgerson.*

… the sky is crowded with other downward-looking satellites, some owned by private intelligence companies. One of these, BlackSky, uses those satellites to feed into a system that's essentially Sentient's unclassified doppelgänger.

When two oil tankers were attacked in the Strait of Hormuz on June 13th, BlackSky's program sent its satellites into action and took pictures of the incident while smoke from the explosions was still spiraling skyward. The ships' drifting beacons and local news reports hinted that something was up, prompting BlackSky analysts to turn their attention to the busy shipping lane near Iran.

Source: It's Sentient–the classified artificial brain developed by US Intelligence

Yes, these are not only self-thinking and future-predicting AI systems, but entire satellites and weapon systems are already equipped with them! The future dreamed up in the Terminator movies of the 80s and 90s is already here as a potentiality.

If you've seen the Netflix show "Black Mirror", you might have thought it's also a sci-fi show, but it's more of a documentary with the purpose of introducing already existing technologies and developments to you, in the guise of "fiction".

The creation of a **mirror-world** is supported by AI Programs that are learning more about us than even our closest friends know. One App, for example, is called Replika. It has been downloaded tens of millions of times since 2017. Quoted from an article titled The App that is trying to replicate you:

*Replika launched in March. At its core is a messaging app where **users spend tens of hours answering questions to build a digital library of information about themselves.** That library is run through a neural network **to create a bot, that in theory, acts as the user would.** Right now, it's just a fun way for people to see how they sound in messages to others, synthesizing the thousands of messages you've sent into a distillate of your tone—rather like an extreme version of listening to recordings of yourself. But its creator, a San Francisco-based startup called Luka, sees a whole bunch of possible uses for it: a digital twin to serve as a companion for the lonely, a living memorial of the dead, created for those left behind, or even, one day, a* version of ourselves that can carry out all the mundane tasks that we humans have to do, but never want to.

*Luka's vision for Replika is **to create a digital representation of you that can act as you would in the world,** dealing with all those inane but time-consuming activities like scheduling appointments and tracking down stuff you need. It's an exciting version of the future, a sort of utopia where bots free us from the doldrums of routine or stressful conversations, allowing us to spend more time being productive, or pursuing some higher meaning.*

The team worked with psychologists to figure out how to make its bot ask questions in a way that would get people to open up and answer frankly. You are free to be as verbose or as curt as you'd like, but the more you say, the greater opportunity the bot has to learn to respond as you would.

A similar app was also portrayed in "Westworld Season 2". Again, these type of apps were invented before the show was even written.

On a bright note: As powerful as all of this *data-amassing* and *behavior-predicting* can be, I don't think it supersedes

a) the power of intention,

b) the power of intuition and

c) the power of spirit.

If all meteorologists, with their masses of data, science and facts, predict that it's going to rain and I intend and pray for sunshine, then all the data is for nothing. I've in fact done this so often (see linked article), that I now tell people "An App does not decide what the weather is like. You have the power to ask for better". Most people think I am joking (that's how far away they are from *Source*). Expected outcomes can be defied with spiritual power. Spirit over matter, spirit over data. That's why I will keep teaching *Reality Creation*, which is the opposite of living so robotically that you succumb to computer-predicted patterns for your life.

13

Fear Of Covid-19 Caused By Lies And Inattentiveness

Dear Powers that be,

I'm trying to be a responsible citizen and follow all of your Covid-rules, but with all due respect, you need to **get your story straight**. Otherwise, the sheep are going to get suspicious.

For example, your recent headlines about Maggie Keenan being the first person to take the brand new Covid vaccine. This woman was already featured in October as being the first person to get a vaccine shot. When I wrote the first draft of this article a week ago, the video was available on this page. Today, I'm looking over this article again, and the video has been removed from the page. It was a video featuring Maggie Keenan and the announcer's words "the first coronavirus vaccine to the UK". The Video was uploaded October 22, 2020, long before it was widely announced that there would be a vaccine and that it would be delivered to the UK and that the first person to receive it would be Maggie Keenan. Removing a video that was seen by Millions, makes you look even more guilty.

Covid-19 vaccine: First person receives Pfizer jab in UK

🕐 08 December 2020   UK

01:20

Margaret Keenan was given the vaccine by May Parsons, matron at University Hospital in Coventry

A UK grandmother has become the first perso the world to be given the Pfizer Covid-19 jab a part of a mass vaccination programme.

ⓘ   cnn.com

Live TV

Faulty US Covid-19 respons meant 130,000 to 210,000 avoidable deaths, report fin

By Maggie Fox, CNN

Updated 1:42 PM EDT, Thu October 22, 2020

CORONAVIRUS PANDEMIC
UK PATIENTS NOW FIRST IN WORLD TO GET AUTHORIZED COVID VACCINE

(CNN) — The Trump Administration's faltering response to the coronavirus pandemic has led to anywhere between 130,000 and 210,000 deaths could have been prevented, according to a repor released Thursday by a team of disaster prepared experts.

As a citizen of the world with little access to quality-information, what are we supposed to think? Did Maggie get the first vaccine shot, twice? Or was the whole thing filmed and prepared well in advance of public announcement? Is she a paid actress posing in a staged event?

Get your story straight, it's embarrassing!

And what of the footage you showed us from China, way back in March 2020, when Coronavirus first broke out? It was horrifying. People **foaming at the mouth, shaking and collapsing in the middle of the streets. Infected Nurses violently convulsing in their hospitals. And then, a whole city emptied as people in space-suits carpet sprayed the**

whole place. Whatever happened to that? Why haven't we seen those kinds of events ever since?

Why didn't that script make it overseas? Where were the foaming-at-the-mouth street-collapsing people in Italy and New York? Were these paid actors playing out scenes meant to instill fear?

In movie-making, this is called "error in continuity". It's when the next scene or episode is not consistent with the previous one. This is why professional movie making has special staff that take care of continuity.

Dear powers that be, you could have solved this weird incongruency by saying that the virus got weaker as it travelled to other countries. But you didn't want to say that, because it wouldn't have scared enough people into submission, right? The death statistics for the U.S. in 2020 are no more or less than any other year. That's a fact.

Granted, maybe your virus is real. But perhaps it's being exaggerated so that you can exploit it for some ulterior agenda?

I wonder why Covid so rapidly declined in China that only a few months later you had stadiums packed with hundreds of thousands of people, giving no care about social distancing–while the rest of the world went into second and third lockdowns?

Is China ever going to be held accountable for faking their Covid Data, as seen in this article and this one? I'm not asking for sanctions, but at the very least, there could have been formal condemnations. Why were numbers downplayed in China and spiked in other countries?

Why are you giving us rules that are far more damaging than the virus itself? If Coronavirus only kills the elderly (but even then, in rare cases), why not focus on the protection of the elderly, rather than putting hundreds of millions of people out of business? You know that the combo of poverty and lack of social contact is much more damaging than this virus. Why is your global messaging ignoring the successful path the Swedes took in having no lockdowns, instead protecting the elderly?

Are you testing how easy it is to make people comply? Is this some kind of mass-scale social experiment? We have given up the two pillars of human well-being: Social Community and economy. I'm amazed that you got most people to comply that easily. Very impressive.

But I think you're getting lazy and people are starting to notice discrepancies. I was at first on the fence, but the more I see, the more I am becoming a Covid-skeptic.

Elon Musk ✓
@elonmusk

Something extremely bogus is going on. Was tested for covid four times today. Two tests came back negative, two came back positive. Same machine, same test, same nurse. Rapid antigen test from BD.

6:47 PM · Nov 13, 2020 · Twitter for iPhone

Figuring out that something bogus is going on is not rocket science.

I'm willing to believe that our scientists and politicians know what they are doing for the well-being of all. But as of late, your laws and measures have become so heavy-handed, they make me doubt your good intentions.

Is it true that flu rates are down by 98% this winter, as widely claimed? I don't know. I don't trust anything I read online. But I could imagine it's true because I was told by a nurse in a local hospital that *all cases* of flu are to be treated as cases of Covid, "just in case". When I asked to speak to the person who said that (and get a recording of it!), the nurse asked me not to because she would "get in trouble". That's one of those little real-life episodes that make you scratch your head.

A few months ago I was walking in the fields, when I came upon a hiking couple. One of them had passed out from a sun stroke. I was asked to call an ambulance. When I called the Ambulance, I was asked at least 5 questions or more relating to Covid before I could state my reason for calling. "Do you have respiratory problems?"–"Have you had contact with anyone who has had Covid?"–"Are you in Self-Quarantine?" It was as if they had gotten their hospital staff to treat *everything* as potential Covid. For goodness' sake! I thought. I could be calling about an emergency, but they didn't care about my reason for calling, all they cared about is robotically asking me about Covid! The incident upset me. If people are being this robotic, something is amiss. *Robotic behavior stems from intense fear-programming.* People with good intentions do not use fear-programming.

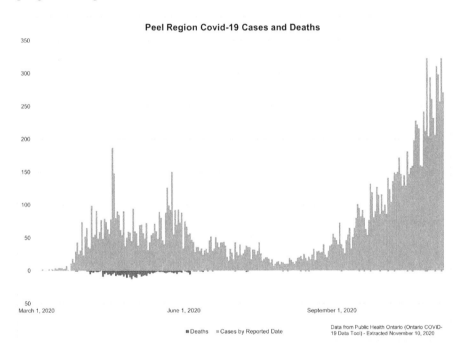

Peel Region Covid-19 Cases and Deaths

Data from Public Health Ontario (Ontario COVID-19 Data Tool) - Extracted November 10, 2020

Why are the reported cases in this instance (Ontario, Canada), skyrocketing, but not the cases of death? Why are false-positives reported by the thousands daily? Why were there so many countries where Covid first broke out in nursing homes, as if planted there?

And what's with the radically Draconian push for *mandatory* vaccination? Just one example: Qantas airlines say that you won't be able to travel if you don't get the vaccine.

What has gotten into these people? **If you are vaccinated, you should have nothing to fear from those who aren't vaccinated, right?** Shouldn't it be every person's responsibility what they put into their body? Should a corporation or Government decide what you must put into your body? Isn't it my body? Aren't you pro-choice?

I wish your talking points on Covid would make sense.

You say lockdowns work, yes? So if lockdowns worked before, why do we need another one? Doesn't the fact that you need another and yet another lockdown prove that the previous lockdowns didn't work? And if they didn't work, what makes you think another one will work?

Heavy-handed measures that defy reason and civil rights make us wonder and view politicians with skepticism. A friend of mine, who disagrees with my views on Covid, says that the lockdowns are good for the environment, they are healing the world. Was that the plan? If so, it's poorly executed.

I'm sorry that many believe that *others* are to blame for their state of health. *"Because someone is not following the rules, we all suffer"*. I've seen a lot of otherwise smart and educated people post that. But it's classic totalitarian thought, a concept used by some of the most inhumane dictatorships n history. The motto is also used by organized crime gangs. *"Because someone is not following the rules, we all suffer"*. At first sight, this tribal thought makes perfect sense. Why does a whole group have to suffer just because one person is acting up? Fortunately, we have laws. But as soon as the "rules" are made up based on fear rather than reason, it turns into:

"Give up your job, your freedom of movement, your freedom of speech, your freedom of association, your family and friends… otherwise I'll get sick."

The better approach is this: **You are responsible for your health, I'm responsible for mine.** If you are fearful about your health, stay inside– but don't force me to. Do you really want to legislate that everyone else gives up their lives because of your private worries? If you're fearful for your health, get vaccinated, but don't force me to.

I'm not afraid of Covid, because I've been paying attention. I've seen the "grown-ups" who are mandating lockdowns, flouting their own lockdown rules. We have seen police officers who are not wearing masks, arresting others for wearing masks. I have seen police officers defying laws and NOT enforcing Covid rules. On the other side, I have seen some breaking into people's homes in SWAT Gear and full body armor just to stop a social gathering. I have seen Italian nurses wearing space-suit like gear and the camera accidentally picking up nearby people not wearing that gear.

The Virus is no probably no Hoax, but the reaction to it is. It's an overreaction. For what? I don't know. Probably the usual: Power and money. Mass-fear-programming always goes back to some megalomaniacs agenda. As for your vaccine: I might take it. I might not. What's it to you? But if it's forced upon me, I will certainly not take it.

14

On The Sexual Misconduct
Of Ancient "Aliens"

You won't read this anywhere else in the world. It's something weird, I discovered while researching my latest book. This is an excerpt from my latest book, Extraterrestrial Linguistics.

—————————

"… Worldwide Linguistic evidence for sexual exploitation through these ancient German speakers. I almost omitted it because it does not paint a flattering image of our spacefaring ancestors. Finally, I decided to include it in the book. My aim is not to worry about cultural sensibilities but to discover our true history, regardless of how it makes anyone look.

I first came across this oddity when I learned, from a Swahili speaking person, that the Swahili word for breast is *Titi*. I thought it might be modern slang or a recent addition to the language from outside. I found that it's neither slang nor modern. It's the official word. A doctor who is saying "Breast Cancer" uses the word *Titi*. Back then, I categorized it as a coincidence. But after my studies for this book, I realize it's not.

I looked up the word "Breast" in many languages. Upon discovering most of them to be *ancient German,* I began looking up other sexual and vulgar terms. After all, sex is timeless to human behavior.

I began by looking up the Amharic (Ethiopian) word for whore, which is *Galemota.* If I separate the word, even a modern German speaker will instantly understand it. *Gale Mota.* In modern German it's "geile Mutter", *Horny Mother* in English.

If that were the only German reference, we could put it off as a fluke, but it's not. The word "horny" itself is *K'enidi,* pronounced Ke-needy. My etymology dictionary says that the English word "Need" is of Germanic origin.

The word for prostitute is *Zimuti Adari.* Again, the German is so pure and well preserved that even modern Germans will understand this ancient tongue. The German word "Mutti" is a variant of 'Mother'. Again! In ancient German it was probably said like this: *Adari Zi Muti,* something like "That is the Mother". Both Ethiopian words Whore and Prostitute point to *different German* words for Mother.

The Amharic word for Love is *Fikiri,* which is ancient German dialect for fucking. In proper Modern German its *"Ficken"*.

The word for breast is *Tuti,* which is close to the German word for "Tits" and similar to the Swahili one.

The Amharic word for bed is *aliga.* I'm looking at this "foreign" language called Amharic, thinking I can't believe it. I rub my eyes and pinch my arm to see if I'm dreaming. In German, "Liege" is actually "bed". Southern German (Bavarian) dialect would precisely say "a Liga" for "a bed".

The word for stupid is *dedebi,* which is De Debi, modern German Depp, which means stupid. I discovered more, but do not wish to reiterate it here. At the very least, this points to the possibility of a group of rather disrespectful ancient German-speaking people for who equate Love with Sex and Mothers with Whores.

So what is going on here? The German was so well preserved that I became suspicious. Could this be a more recent influence? Just to make sure, I checked whether Ethiopia was ever a German colony in the last few hundred years. It wasn't. So how did it get into the language? Or was it there to begin with?

A tribe of people in South Africa who call themselves the Xhosa (pronounced Kosa) also show signs of vulgar ancient German. How these slang-like phrases found their way into an ancient language is a mystery to me.

The word for Whore is *Ihenyukazi*. Kazi is ancient German for Kitten or "Pussy".

Ubufozi is the Xhosa word for Vagina. *Fotze* is vulgar German for "cunt". In the language of the Zulu tribe, the same word, *Ubufozi*, refers to femininity. To show the global reach of these ancients: All the way across the world, on the Pacific Island of Samoa, the word for Vagina is *Fusi*. That's essentially the same sound. How is that possible? It can only be explained if this variant of ancient German was, at one time, global or these tribes wandered the entire globe.

Food is *Ukutya*, ancient German *Kut, Ya*. In English, that means "it's good, yes". Isn't that ridiculous? You say "the food is good, yes", and it's recorded to be the translation for "food".

Breast *Ibele*, Bele is ancient German for Balls.

Bed is *Ibhedi* Bed-hi, which is ag. German dialect for going to bed.

Woman—*Umfazi*, which is again, *Fotze*, vulgar and derogatory German for "Cunt".

The phenomenon is not limited to African languages, it can be found across the world.

The Basque term for Whore is *Urdanga*. *Dan* is ancient German. for lady and *Ur* is probably not the same as the German "Ur" (origin), but the German *Hur* (Whore). Ur-danga then, is *Hur-Dan-Ga*, the ancient German word "whore-lady".

The Estonian word for fuck is *Hoorama*, which is the ancient German "*Hur Rama* ", to "ram a whore".

The Maori word for vagina is *puta tenetene.* Pute is Latin for "girl" and also ancient German for "whore".

————————-

It's difficult to put all of this off as "coincidence". Especially in combination with all the other linguistic evidence presented in the book. But what on Earth does it mean? Was there a gang of ancient German-speaking people that travelled the whole world? And if so, why are they absent from history books?

Or is it that these words originally had no negative connotation? That's also a possibility, I guess. In Arabic, the word Hoor refers to the most pure and beautiful women in Heaven. Could it be that "the fallen ones", knew that the Hoor are the purest women in Heaven and wished to desecrate the word to mean the opposite of "pure"? Maybe.

What if I told you that, *approximately 1000 years ago, a band of misogynistic German-speaking people in flying saucers roamed the Earth to sexually exploit and abuse surface-dwellers?* You'd probably think it sounds insane. It wouldn't fit to anything you think you "know" about History. And it would also require giving up too many cherished beliefs, not just one:

The belief that flying saucers don't exist and, if they do, only exist since recently.

The belief that ancient aliens are actually "aliens".

The belief that our own technology began with the industrial revolution 200 years ago.

The belief that humans haven't been to deep space.

The belief that school teaches a fairly accurate account of history.

The belief that technologically advanced people are benevolent.

But if you've read the book, the utter strangeness of the statement is reduced one level. If you take an unbiased look at ancient mythology, you'll see that the writings are rife with the sexual exploitation and misconduct by beings mistaken to be "the gods".

From the Book of Genesis, Chapter 6, verse 4:

"There were giants on the earth in those days, and also afterward, when the sons of God came in to the daughters of men and they bore children to them. Those were the mighty men who were of old, men of renown. Then the LORD saw that the wickedness of man was great upon the earth, and that every inclination of the thoughts of his heart was altogether evil all the time,"

The Hebrew word for Giants is "Nephilim". Who are these Nephilim who came down to Earth and had sex with human women?

As shown in the book, the word "Ilim" or "Elim" refers to higher beings. Ne-philim could therefore be a negation, as in Not-Elim. That would fit to the notion that they are "fallen angels". But that's only speculation on my part.

The Book of Numbers, Chapter 13, verse 13, has another name for them:

"We even saw the Nephilim there–the descendants of Anak that come from the Nephilim! We seemed like grasshoppers in our own sight, and we must have seemed the same to them!"

As explained in my book, the word "An" is a worldwide term, used in every language, to denote *Ancestors*. It's preserved in modern German as the same word, *Ahnen*. Even the Sumerian word Annunaki, which "ancient aliens" researchers claim refers to extraterrestrials, contains the

An. As you learn in the book, the word "Ak" or "Ok" refers to a specific star constellation. An-Ak are "the ancestors from Ak".

But it gets even stranger. If you wish to know how strange, you can read it in my book "Extraterrestrial Linguistics".

15

The Mandela Effect
and Reality Creation

Today I remember putting my sneakers into the trunk of the car, for a later activity. I noticed they were filthy. I had an appointment, so there was no time to clean them or get others. I could clean them later. I went to my appointment. Afterwards, I went to get my sneakers out of the trunk and they were completely clean. Spotless.

What? How? Am I delusional? False memory? Or did I switch timelines, from one parallel world to another? I believe we jump timelines. I wrote a book called Parallel Universes of Self about this in 2006. I think this happens more often than we notice.

If you can shift timelines toward a reality change, as if an event never happened, it stands to reason that the *world* can do it too.

I clearly remember Gibraltar as an Island between Morocco and Spain. I remember that the "Straits of Gibraltar" were two waterways on either side of the Island. I remember that the Island, under British rule, was not populated and merely had one or two facilities on it. It was just a piece of rock in the Ocean.

Looking at the Map today, this is not the case:

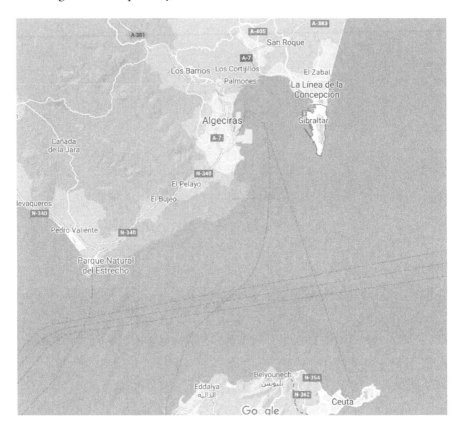

Gibraltar is not an Island, it's attached to Spain. It's not even directly between Morocco and Spain, as I thought it was. And it's more than a small piece of rock, it has a population and even a mountain on it. It looks nothing like the Gibraltar I remember.

You could say my memory is tricking me or I was misinformed about Gibraltar. But to me, that sounds offensive. Granted, I have never been to Gibraltar, I can only recount what I was shown on film, taught in school and read in books. I lived in a parallel world where Gibraltar was in the middle of the *Straits* of Gibraltar (plural), not at the side of the singular *Strait* of Gibraltar.

This is called "The Mandela Effect", deriving from the fact that some people remember Mandela dying in prison in the 1980s while others insist he died in 2013.

Over the years people have asked me why I haven't written about the Mandela Effect, as it ties in nicely with Parallel Universes. The reason is this: It's a *nerdy* subject. By that, I mean, there is a lot of thinking and speculation, but little practical application in the context of *Parallel Universes Coaching.* I wrote my 2006 book Parallel Universes with *practical* self-improvement in mind.

The term *Mandela Effect* gained traction around 2013, when Mandela died:

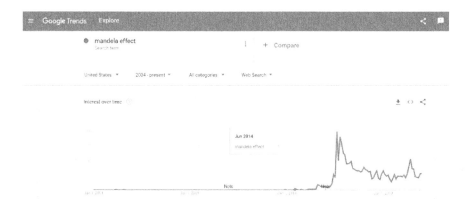

Some things ascribed to this effect appear to be about remembering things inaccurately, but others appear to prove genuine parallel worlds. Usually these two views are separated into two camps, the naysayers vs. the believers, but such divided camps are for people who lack the power of discernment. If one is too lazy to look deeper, then everything is explained from only one viewpoint and that's how these "camps" are established.

The Mandela Effect is fascinating, but of what practical use is it to puzzle over various trivia? Thinking about it more deeply, I found one way in which it is useful: It can shake up "everything you believe to be true". It awakens us to life being more mysterious and interesting than commonly assumed.

I think it's good to shake up peoples belief-system. Like I did with my recent book "Extraterrestrial Linguistics ". It's good to entertain the idea that *everything* you believe is unreal. Why is that good? Because it trains you to think outside of habitual boxes. The mind seeks comfort in the familiar, in "consensus-reality'. To consider things that nobody else is believing, helps you grow.

Remember: Just because you *entertain* an idea, doesn't mean you have to believe in it. I entertain all kinds of "crazy" ideas, as a matter of training. It doesn't mean I buy into them fully. I savor the belief for some time before either swallowing it or spitting it out. Embracing or rejecting an unusual idea before savoring it, is the root of ignorance. The difference between me and crazy people is that I am fully aware of what "normal" people believe.

But even more useful than reading examples of changed History or the Mandela effect, is to **create your own preferred timeline**. Your own amazing life can be created regardless of where Gibraltar is or what else is happening in the world. The Universe will keep teaching you that your life is up to you and can be turned around at any minute. And did you know that the way you see world events is a reflection of the way you see yourself? Do you see world events or the Mandela Effect as mysterious and amazing? That's because *you are.*

"But Fred, global Covid Pandemic is not the timeline I wanted! And it affects me! It's not true that I choose my preferred reality! I am dependent on the worlds political reality!"

Well, if you say so. Guess what–it hasn't affected me negatively so far. 2020 was my best year financially and in health. And I also happen to be living in parts of the world without lockdown or mask mandate. So I never experienced any of the consequences of Covid (even though I have written several articles objecting to the politics around it). If you really think all that is a coincidence, you don't know Reality Creation.

Here's how to make the Mandela Effect more of a practical experience: Notice errors in continuity in your own life, especially after a radical change in energy-state or self-image. When you shift your state rapidly, then the new-you is not living on the same timeline as the old-you. Pay attention and you'll notice the changes. Things are not as fixed as they seem.

16

The U.s. Owns Patents For Flying Saucers That Can Travel Air, Land And Water

In my recent book <u>Extraterrestrial Linguistics</u>, I showed how flying saucers and flying triangles have been used by **Human** Beings for hundreds, even thousands of years. They have been sighted in space, air, land and underwater. They have been chronicled, drawn, painted, etched and written about. Flying saucers or "UFOs" have **also** been **human made** in the last 50 years, as I show in my recent write-up titled <u>Human Made Flying Saucers</u>.

The U.S. Government has not only been well aware of "UFOs", they have been manufacturing them!

Quoting from an article titled ""<u>Navy got 'UFO Patent' granted by warning of similar Chinese Tech Advances</u>".

The United States Secretary of Navy is listed as the assignee on several radical aviation technologies patented by an aerospace engineer working at the Naval Air Warfare Center Aircraft Division (NAWCAD) headquarters in Patuxent River, Maryland. One of these patents describes a "hybrid aerospace-underwater craft" claimed to be capable of truly extraordinary feats of speed and maneuverability in air, water, and outer space alike thanks to a revolutionary electromagnetic propulsion system.

Sound far fetched? You're not alone.

A primary patent examiner at the United States Patent and Trademark Office (USPTO) thought so too. But then the Chief Technical Officer (CTO) of the Naval Aviation Enterprise personally wrote a letter addressed to the examiner claiming that the U.S. needs the patent as the Chinese are already "investing significantly" in these aerospace technologies that sound eerily similar to the UFOs reported by Navy pilots in now well-known encounters.

…

Pais is named as the inventor on four separate patents for which the U.S. Navy is the assignee: a curiously shaped "High Frequency Gravitational Wave Generator;" a room temperature superconductor; an electromagnetic 'force field' generator that could deflect asteroids; and, perhaps the strangest of all, one titled "Craft Using An Inertial Mass Reduction Device." While all are pretty outlandish-sounding, the latter is the one that the Chief Technical Officer of the Naval Aviation Enterprise personally vouched for in a letter to the USPTO, claiming the Chinese are already developing similar capabilities.

The patent was first applied for on April 28, 2016, over a decade after the Nimitz Carrier Strike Group encountered strange Tic Tac-shaped aircraft and nearly a year after Navy pilots across multiple squadrons flying out of Naval Air Station Oceana and NAS Norfolk experienced a string of bizarre encounters with unidentified aircraft, some of which, like the Tic Tac, seemed to possess exotic performance capabilities.

To read the rest of the long article click the link above.

Even though the patents were filed recently (2016), I know "the Government" has had these devices for a long time. They're only pretending to *just* have discovered them. They hope to make these look like "new inventions", hoping nobody will notice.

These "new patens" are nothing new. The Saucer UFO has been sighted since the 1930s and the Triangle "UFO" has been sighted since at least the 1980s in modern times (and hundreds to thousands of years ago, according to my book).

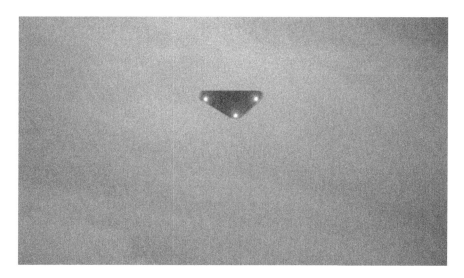

I guess it's good news for us, if the public becomes aware of more advanced technology. It's about time.

Quoting from another article "What's going on with UFOs and the Department of Defense?"

"… *cryptic statements made by top players in the dark areas of aerospace development, such as those of the late Ben Rich, a Lockheed's Skunk Works chief that is largely credited for giving birth to stealth technology as we know it today. For instance, Rich told Popular Mechanics the following that underscores just how long major breakthroughs in man-made clandestine aerospace technology can stay hidden:*

"There are some new programs, and there are certain things, some of them 20 or 30 years old, that are still breakthroughs and appropriate to keep quiet about [because] other people don't have them yet."

Hypersonics, drone swarms, directed energy weapons, and a full-on emerging arms race in space are just some of the very real activities and technologies that will dominate the near future of American weapons development. The products of all of these initiatives, once manifested, could appear positively alien to curious bystanders.

Before shouting "aliens", don't underestimate what humans can do and have **already** done. Sure, it's possible that we had the assistance of aliens to build these devices. The Universe is full of aliens. But are aliens really required to explain "UFOs", in this case? All evidence considered, it's more likely that flying saucers and triangles have been **humans** all along.

17

Four Amazing Things About Washington D.c. You Didn't Learn In School

These are four fascinating things about Washington D.C. that you didn't learn in school and won't find on Wikipedia. For thousands of years, the ruling classes of Earth have operated from metaphysical and spiritual ideas and withheld much of it from the public.

I realize there is much more to say about Washington DC and the layout and symbolism of its city streets and parks and obelisks and pyramids and whatnot. But that's already been said on thousands of other websites. I limit this article to things *even less known* or shown anywhere.

1. Washington D.C. was dedicated to Virgin Mary, then to the goddess Columbia.

History is the struggle between different spiritual influences. There has been a Being, appearing since hundreds of years, claiming to be Virgin Mary. This Being performs paranormal acts, provides warnings, heals and makes predictions. This Being has been known for asking people to *dedicate specific places*, towns, cities and even countries to her. If they are "consecrated to her", this would bring the region her blessing. See, for example, the book "The Great Apparitions of Mary", psychic

Government spy Ingo Swann (yes, the Government paid spies to spy for them psychically).

It appears that the founders of the United States had this in mind, when they placed their Capital right in between Virginia and Maryland, making it "Virgin Mary Land". From all we know about the spiritual attitudes of early Americans, the names of these states are hardly a coincidence.

In 1801 however, the city was *removed* from Virginia-Maryland when a new federal district was created, the district of Columbia, so named after the <u>goddess Columbia</u>. From that point forward, a new supernatural deity was in charge of the city. According to her Wikipedia page, in early times she was....

"... depicted as a woman who was only partly dressed, typically in bright feathers, which invariably formed her headdress. She often held a parrot, was seated on an alligator, with a cornucopia (symbolizing wealth). Sometimes a severed head was a further attribute, or in prints scenes of cannibalism were seen in the background."

2. Washington D.C. was originally designed to be a miniature replica of the USA.

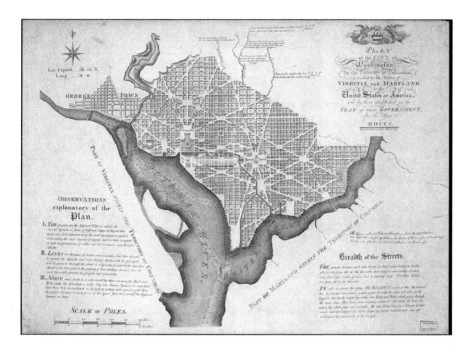

The image above is the <u>L'Enfant Plan</u>, so named after the first mayor of Washington D.C. who developed the city on orders of the first President, George Washington. This final plan was drawn up by Andrew Ellicott.

Tilt your head slightly to the right and you can see that the city layout is meant to be a miniature replica of the United States of America.

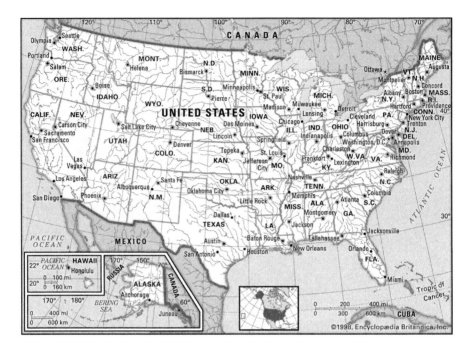

Yes, this is just me speculating. I have no evidence. But examine the upper city limits for a moment. And then compare them to the northern Border of the United States of America. Then try the west coast, upper left of Washington D.C. Then the East Coast. It's uncanny, isn't it? It's strange how the shape of the bordering rivers perfectly align with the east and west coast.

It wouldn't be much of a surprise. The maker of D.C. was obviously into metaphysical geometry. People like this are fond of "as above, so below, as in the big, so in the small. They like replicas and miniatures. If Washington D.C. was to represent the U.S. A, then it could also represent it in shape, they perhaps thought. Not that you'll find *any* mention of this in school or college textbooks.

3. The District of Columbia is not part of any U.S. State and not subject to U.S. Law

Even though physically, the city is in Virginia and Maryland, the District of Columbia is legally not part of the United States of America, because it is not a state. It is therefore not subject to the law of the United States of America, but has its own. It is a separate entity, put above the states as their Capitol. Residents of Washington D.C. have no representation in the Senate.

The idea behind this is, presumably, that in order to rule a country, one must be above that country.

In this sense, Washington D.C. is similar to the City of London, which is not governed by Great Britain and the Vatican, which is not governed by Italy. Each of these have their famous dome shaped buildings, perhaps not coincidentally.

| Vatican | London | Washington DC |

Oddly enough, the Pentagon (Military) is located outside the official lines of the District of Columbia, and yet their post office addresses are named as being within the District of Columbia.

4. The U.S. Capitol appears to be built atop an unknown and mysterious pillared structure

The construction consulting company GEI, that in 2003 helped build the visitors center at the Capitol Building in Washington D.C., shows an astonishing photo of excavation work. I'm putting a screenshot, directly from their website, here (as of today):

97

GEI provided excavation support and geotechnical consulting and proposed a revised construction sequence that saved the design build team millions of dollars.

When I first saw this, I was surprised. I had never seen the Capitol Building this way. It felt like it's underbelly had been stripped naked, revealing something unexpected. This is what it normally looks like, when there is no construction work:

Another angel of the excavated pillars below the Capitol:

What is that pillar structure below the Capitol entrance? What are those pillars below the... pillars? Some older building that the Capitol was built on top of? Some kind of hidden Temple? An ancient Government building? An unknown basement? I spent an hour searching online for a reasonable explanation and found none.

The page is, as far as I can tell, the only source for these images. More strangely, if you look at the pillars closely, you can see that they appear to be a continuation of the structures above, which are the stairs flanked by large cubes. It almost looks as if the Capitol building was at one point much higher and part of it had been buried underground. Or as if parts of the old structure had been broken away when a new one was built on top of it.

The pillars are not the only thing striking. The rest of the underground structure is covered but appears to be architecturally aligned with the structure above. Compare top and bottom in this area, for example. It is indented at the same spots the upper, visible part of the structure is indented.

Maybe this is just how the base of the building was built. But common sense would tell us it's too elaborate to be a base.

My curious self would like to know, but I didn't find the original construction plans. I found a page that contains floor plans, including basement plans of the Capitol, but nothing pointing to this kind of depth and height shown by the columns. When I search on Capitol basement, I receive areas of a much lower ceiling. What you will find is that there are miles of tunnels below the Capitol, leading to other buildings in Washington DC, as well as a private subway system only used by members of Congress.

Untapped New York by Augustin Pasquet

The Capitol building is the worlds most famous symbol of Democracy. Even if the mysterious structure below it turns out to have a mundane explanation: I bet you never guessed that this is what it looks like beneath.

It's amazing how much you can see if you stop taking things for granted and have a closer look at them.

18

The Many Fake Selves
And The Real Self

Have you ever felt awkward meeting a person you know in an unfamiliar context?

How does it feel to run across your boss in the Sauna?

Or to meet your employee in the supermarket?

Or to see your basketball buddies, that you've only seen in sports-gear, wearing suit and tie?

Or to come across your teenage son hanging out with friends in the park?

Or to visit your spouse at work?

Does that feel awkward? For most people it does.

The reason is that we play many roles. These are fake selves. I don't mean that negatively. Fake selves *serve* the purpose of experiencing specific realities. The "father self" is to raise a child, the "lover self" is to please the wife, the "boss self" is the one put on in the office and the "friend self" he puts on with his buddies. Each of these selves have certain voices, gestures, clothes, mannerisms, vocabulary and activities. The lover-self wears perfume, the father self probably doesn't. The boss self gives orders, the friend self probably doesn't, unless identities get mixed up.

The true self is none of these. That's why it feels awkward when they mix. That's why he doesn't want his wife to go to the pub with him, because there he is not being "lover self" but "friend self". He does not like kissing his wife when his son is near, even though his son is an adult, because his lover self and father self are separate.

But the more authentic a person becomes, the less contrast there is between the parts. Then, his son, his wife, his employees and his buddies can all sit at the same table and he'll feel comfortable. That's not to say that he'll talk in the same way to his employees as with his buddies, son or wife. But if he's authentic, he'll feel fine having different realities present.

At a recent dinner, the host said to us "I've only invited anti-vaxxers, so everyone can speak freely". It felt like some kind of underground resistance meeting. I wouldn't define myself as an "anti vaxxer". I think vaccines are fine. Just because I *once* wrote an article criticizing *mandatory* vaccines, the host assumed "he is an anti-vaxxer". I guess people like pegging others. The conversation didn't go anywhere, because everyone was agreeing on everything. Echo Chamber. I'd find it much more fun had there been a diversity of opinion. Nobody needs to be protected from other peoples opinions.

A picture of earth before and after your opinion

Truth does not mind being questioned, and a lie does not like being challenged.

It's happened several times that I sat in an airport and met people who were flying to or from my seminars. At first, I didn't like that. I was in "relaxing and minding my business" mode, not in "Public Speaker" mode. People came and asked me for autographs or other stuff. Some were polite and soon moved on. But others simply assumed that, because they read my books, we were now friends and they could sit and chat.

Today, the same scenario does not bother me, because I no longer feel the need to entertain. I can sit at ease and don't need a witty answer to everything, nor do I have to be clean shaven and smartly dressed. Life is much easier without fake identities. If I dress smartly, it's because I like to, not to impress others. That's not to say that I'd get so relaxed that I'd go on an all-night drinking spree with them. But regardless of whether I am with family, friends, readers, fans, students or business partners I am the same person.

A while back I noticed that I was putting more effort into talking to my spouse, when other people are present. That's inauthentic, and I'm glad I caught it. If I'm alone with my wife in the car, I might comment on a slow driver in front of me: "… wut da heck". When someone else is present, I'll say this instead: "What a beautiful new bridge they built over there. Has anyone walked it yet?" This is typical, as we usually like to put on a polite, sociable face in front of strangers. So I have practiced to put a little more wakefulness into my speech, even when no one is watching. Not to impress anyone, but because I like to speak consciously. Lazy speech is only a habit.

Yesterday I slept at a farm far out in the wilderness with a group of friends. After a barbecue, we spent a tranquil evening chatting, and all people went to bed by midnight. Everything was quiet and peaceful. Then, at 3:30 a.m. the peace was abruptly torn through by loud banging noises. I was startled awake. It was a friend of mine, chopping wood with full force, looking like a madman in the moonlight. He then carried the wood into a sauna and lit it. I liked the fact that he was being authentic. He didn't care what we thought of the fact that he was going to the Sauna at 3:30. But mixed into his authenticity was a lack of respect. It would never occur to me to make noise at while everyone is sleeping. Most people would be mindful of others. Once you find your true self, take good care to balance your newfound authenticity with respect toward others.

One of the most inauthentic type of identities is the so-called "spiritual identity". Some people, who have read my books on higher states of consciousness, expect me to have a "spiritual identity", meaning an extremely narrow band of behavior that is stereotypical and boring. Recently, I purchased a rough looking, lifted off-road car, like something out of Mad Max. Someone commented: "*I wouldn't have expected that from a spiritual person* ". The comment amazed me. It reveals a cliche image of a "spiritual person". So what kind of car is a "spiritual person" supposed to drive? A humble car that draws no attention to itself? Life is polarity. A person can be generally humble but at other times, expressive. What's next? Should I never wear jeans but only loose white robes? Should I have no playful side, no weird side and just be dull and boring and only talk about "being in the now" all the time? Being spiritual and having a spiritual identity are two very different things. A person of high consciousness is multi-faceted. That person can playfully occupy many roles, without fully buying into any of them. You are much, much more than a single identity, much more than an astrological definition, much more than how others define you, much more than you think. You are full of unexpected and surprising sides. And as you become authentic, you will allow yourself to explore more of self and also allow others to show more of who they are.

There is a public thought and a private thought. Authenticity means that they get closer over time until they become one.

19

Why It's Empowering
To Talk Less

"In the beginning was the word, and the word was with God, and the word was God."

John 1:1

"All of our problems stem from our inability to sit quietly in a room alone,"

Blaise Pascal

"Your word is your wand. The game of life is a boomerang. Our thoughts, words and deeds return to us sooner or later, with astounding accuracy,"

Florence Scovel Shinn

"The internal dialogue is what grounds people in the daily world. The world is such-and-such and so and so only because we talk to ourselves about it being such-and-such and so and so."

Carlos Castaneda

The life you experience, is a mirror of what you talked about. You have *talked your life into existence.* Your words are energy and creative power, and if you knew that, you would choose your verbal output more

109

consciously. "In the beginning was the word, and the word was with the Creator and *the word was the Creator".*

Talking too much is disempowering because it's creating too much. If you put too many images on a canvas, you do not manifest a clear picture and the space looks crowded. But if you put only one image, one word on the canvas, it manifests clearly. If you could speak an intention, without following it with dozens of contradicting thoughts, it would manifest instantly. That's what my 2008 book "The Reality Creation Technique" is about.

Too much input is an obstruction to word-power. At the hairdressers recently, I counted at least 10 sources of verbal input and imagery. There were two TVs running and also a radio playing music. There were six hairdressers, chatting away incessantly. It's safe to say that not much is manifested in such an environment. Too many thoughts are accumulated, so no single thought can manifest. So many unrelated, random and disparate thoughts are spoken, then the word loses its manifesting power. And it's a good thing we don't have manifesting power in such a state, otherwise we'd manifest chaos. So not only negative thinking hinders manifestation but also too much thinking.

As a Coach, my main job is to listen. Sometimes I'll ask a question, not because I don't know the answer, but to direct the persons attention to pertinent things. If I don't say too much, the little that I say, will have greater impact. If I were to talk all the time, none of what I say would be taken all that important.

Over-talking is one of the human weaknesses. In the past, I've had students who don't stop talking unless asked to. If I were to just sit and observe quietly, they'd talk without interruption, hopping from topic to topic. Sometimes over-talking devolves into complaint. As a coach, I am in the Business of helping a person examine their thoughts. But if they talk too much, there is not much time left for thought-examination. It's a cup of tea overflowing. The cup is full, but some keep pouring tea, without tasting, consuming or experiencing the tea already poured. It's similar to continually eating, without digesting what was eaten. The reason some people talk and complain continually, is because they do not wish to feel. That's because they are not doing what they prefer in life and do not wish to confront or feel that fact. And so they create, create, create and keep creating, much more than they can digest.

Some people talk about what they *will* do, some just do it. In fact, if someone talks too much about what they *will* do, chances are that they won't. I've observed this many times. If you were going to do it, you wouldn't have to talk about it that much.

You have two ears and one mouth, because listening should be double the amount of speaking. There are, in fact, four ways of dealing with words and talking is only *one* of them:

1. Listening

2. Reading

3. Writing

4. Talking

I recommend you listen more than you speak and read more than you write. For every book I write, I read about 30. Before I speak for 10 minutes, I have listened for 30 minutes.

Question: If you have nothing good to say, why say anything at all? When you talk, don't you wish it to be useful and uplifting. Putting your words to good use, means to inform, entertain, teach, charm. If you talk in a happy mood, your talk makes others happy. Such talk differs from the random chatter and gossip so many engage in. Negative ways of talking are mostly learned on TV and in Movies. While you grow up, you see people talking a certain way on screen and you think this is the way people talk. Then you imitate that. If you've ever caught yourself talking like some character on your favorite shows, you know this is true. Many movies feature much more talking than happens in real life, giving people the impression that it's not "normal" or "ok" to be silent with people. But it's entirely fine. There is energy and vibratory communication that is beyond words. It can be felt when two people are silent in the same room. When they are silent, their energies synchronize.

You see me talking a lot in Seminars and Videos. But in my private life, I don't talk much. Often, I'll talk out of politeness, because people think it's "weird" if a person just sits there in silence. My talking less does not come from inhibition, it comes from a calm no-mind state. I know my words have creative power, so I aspire to use my voice wisely. The more calm your mind, the more easily your speech manifests. Therefore, the more deeply calm and authentic you become, the more you will want to choose words more consciously.

20

Why Are Terror Attacks Simulated In Training Exercises Before They Happen?

In *Reality Creation Coaching,* I ask students to simulate or act-out a desired reality before it happens. This energetically sets the stage for the real thing happening, it invokes it. Only success attracts success, so if you want something to manifest, let it happen beforehand.

Is it possible that there's a dark variation of this technique? Almost all large-scale "terrorist attacks" are simulated or acted out in role-play before they actually happen. What follows are just a few examples, quoted from mainstream news:

Hours Before the Terror Attacks, Paris Practiced for a Mass Shooting -13 Nov 2015–*17 Nov 2015–Since the Charlie Hebdo attacks in January… Paris-area ambulance crews and emergency personnel have taken part in regular exercises designed to test their readiness for possible attacks. One such exercise was held on Friday morning, the day of the latest terror attacks. In a twist of fate, the simulated emergency was a mass shooting, according to Dr. Mathieu Raux, emergency room chief at the Pitié-Salpetrière hospital in Paris. During Friday's exercise, trauma specialists used a centralized dispatch system to set priorities and direct victims to the ER best equipped to treat their injuries. Ambulance services made sure they were ready to roll, and* *hospitals verified that surgeons and staff could be quickly summoned to treat arriving victims. "We tested every link in the chain," Raux said. Because Paris emergency physicians work 24-hour shifts, virtually every ER doctor on duty in the city Friday night had already taken part in the exercise earlier that day.*

Source: <u>Bloomberg–Hours Before the Terror Attacks, Paris Practiced for a Mass Shooting</u>

Hell of a Coincidence–Officers who took down Christchurch gunman were in a training exercise

"... the video shows armed police wrestling a man to the ground in broad daylight on the side of the road. The world now knows it was the man accused of the Christchurch killings. The officers who tracked him down are being described as "heroic". Those two police officers acted with absolute courage," Police Commissioner Mike Bush told media. "I am so proud of what they've done." We now know more about exactly what happened in the moments before, including the fact that the officers were at a training day, preparing for an event like Friday's tragedy. Police Association President Chris Cahill called it a "hell of a coincidence".

Source: <u>Newshub–Christchurch Officers were in Training Exercise</u>

Boston Marathon Bombing "Police response training planned, but bombs hit first,"–April 15, 2013

The scenario had been carefully planned: A terrorist group prepared to hurt vast numbers of people around Boston would leave backpacks filled with explosives at Faneuil Hall, the Seaport District, and in other towns, spreading waves of panic and fear. Detectives would have to catch the culprits.

Months of painstaking planning had gone into the exercise, dubbed "Operation Urban Shield," meant to train dozens of detectives in the Greater Boston area to work together to thwart a terrorist threat...

… But two months before the training exercise was to take place, the city was hit with a real terrorist attack executed in a frighteningly similar fashion. The chaos of the Boston Marathon bombings disrupted plans for the exercise, initially scheduled for this weekend, forcing police to postpone. Now officials must retool aspects of the training.

"The real thing happened before we were able to execute," said a law enforcement official with direct knowledge of the planned exercise.

Source: Boston Globe–Police Response Training Planned but bomb hits first

Coincidence of bomb exercises, London Tube July 7, 2005

It began when Peter Power, one time high ranking employee of Scotland Yard and member of its Anti-Terrorist Branch, reported in two major UK media outlets that his company Visor Consulting had on the morning of 7th of July been conducting 'crisis exercises' whose scenarios uncannily mirrored those of the actual attack.

… the exercises involved 'a thousand people' as well as a dedicated crisis team whose number was not specified. The consultant described the simulation of 'simultaneous attacks on an underground and mainline station' and 'bombs going off precisely at the railway stations' at which the actual bombings occurred.

Source: Channel 4 News–Coincidence of Bomb Exericses

A Simulated Emergency Exercise with High Explosives Stolen in the same County the Next Day–April 17, 2018

On April 17, 2018 the Lancaster County Emergency Management Agencies within 10 miles of the Peach Bottom Atomic Power Station was to participate in a full scale exercise involving a simulated emergency at the plant–On April 18, 640 pounds of high explosives stolen in Lancaster County, Pennsylvania; ATF offers reward.

Source: Local News: Lancaster County to participate in Emergency Exercise

Local News: 640 pounds of high explosives stolen

9/11 Military Drills on terrorist plane Hijackings, 11 September 2001

On September 11, 2001, Operation Northern Vigilance *was a NORAD operation which involved deploying fighter aircraft… in order to simulate a hijacking situation, including terrorist pilots. The operation was one part simulation, one part real world. It was immediately called off after NORAD received word that the Federal Aviation Administration had evidence of a hijacking. All simulated information (so-called "injects") were purged from computer screens at NORAD headquarters in Colorado.*

Aside from military exercises, a National Reconnaissance Office *drill wa*s *being conducted on September 11, 2001. In a simulated event, a small aircraft would crash into one of the towers of the agency's headquarters after experiencing a mechanical failure. The NRO is the branch of the Department of Defense in charge of spy satellites. According to its spokesman Art Haubold: "It was just an incredible coincidence that this happened to involve an aircraft crashing into our facility, as soon as the real-world events began, we canceled the exercise."*

On September 12, 2001, there was due to take place the second part of an exercise known as Operation Tripod, set up to "test the plan to distribute antibiotics to the entire city population during a bioterrorism attack." Richard Sheirer, director of the New York City Mayor's Office of Emergency Management (NYC OEM), had hired "over 1,000 Police Academy cadets and Fire Department trainees to play terrified civilians afflicted with various medical conditions, allergies, and panic attacks."

Source: Wikipedia: Military Drills on 9-11

There are many more, this is not the place to list them all.

What does it mean? We keep hearing what a remarkable "coincidence" it all is. But this "coincidence" is not the exception. Simulated terror attacks almost always accompany real ones. Most of us aren't even aware of this **pattern** because our incompetent mainstream journalists don't show these instances side by side. They say "Wow! What an amazing coincidence!". If it happens three months later, they say: "Wow, what a coincidence! Wild!". I have yet to see them say, "This same thing happened months ago. And a year ago. And 3 years ago. And 4 years ago. Hmmm… maybe there's a pattern here?" If you have the attention-span of a toddler, you'll go "Wow! What an amazing coincidence!" every time it happens.

What does it mean? A few explanations come to mind:

1. By some mysterious cosmic law, every event is foreshadowed before it happens.

2. There are clandestine groups who wish to conjure the real event by visualizing and acting it out beforehand.

3. The exercises are carried out because people get an intuitive foreboding of danger and wish to prepare for it.

The first option assumes a neutral motive, the second one assumes a negative one, and the third a positive one. Or it could be something I am not even thinking of now, because my mind is too small to conceive it. There's no need to decide on a definitive answer. Keeping the question open keeps your mind open.

The first explanation could make sense because events *are* foreshadowed before they happen. Why do you think the word "foreshadow" was invented? When something is about to manifest, there are signs of its coming. Before a storm, there is lightning and thunder. Before a war, there are troop movements. Before you get your big breakthrough success, there are hints that it is going to happen. The foreshadowing explanation does not exclude explanations two and three.

In explanation two, there are a group of people who are artificially and ritualistically create the foreshadow to support the real event. This would mean that terrorist attacks are not what they seem, but "false flags" that benefit a specific agenda. For example, the 9/11 attacks could have been carried out by people eager to invade the middle east, to use as a pretext for that invasion. The pretend-version of the event is then performed by these shadowy people to energetically support the success of their operation. Sound weird? Maybe. But the world is a weird place, is it not?

The third explanation could make sense in that fearful people tend to attract what they are afraid of and act upon. People are scared it's going to happen, they do an exercise to prepare for it, inadvertently helping to manifest what they fear. The fear-waves and actions travel through the ether and influence someone to act out the real thing. If you think this explanation is ridiculous: Don't be so sure. Dogs have been known to attack fearful people and leave those who fear not in peace.

Regardless of which of these three explanations (or a combo of the three) are correct, they all involve *reality creation* dynamics. Seen with a reality creation lens, there is nothing unusual about events being *pretended* before they *happen*. That's expected! I've spent the last 30 years teaching people to prepare for success and to act out what they want before it can happen. That it also works in the negative is unfortunate, but serves as a warning to you: **What are you preparing for in life?** Are you acting upon fear and preparing for the worst, or acting on love and preparing for the best? The question is especially important in these strange times. Are you preparing for the world to get worse, or do you believe it will get better on act-as-if it will get better? The world needs more people acting on good faith, not preparing for doom.

21

The Incomparable

A student was struggling to sell a piece of real estate at the top floor of a high rise building. It had a sky pool and a beautiful outdoor veranda overlooking the city. There was a granite-slab that ran from the room out onto a lounge-like veranda. It was used as a long dining or party table. It had a high ceiling and panoramic windows around the building. It was one very large room with a small chamber and bathroom in the center. And it had no kitchen, even though a kitchen could be installed. The problem? It wasn't normal. *Too* unique.

Incomparable.

After futile selling attempts, he asked me for advice. I told him to package it differently. So he staged it with beautiful colored lights running along the Veranda, like something out of *Miami Vice*. When people came for viewing, he added finger foods on the granite slab, to point out that it's a table. Soft lounge music was playing. Viewing times were in the evening, because it looked much better with the city lights on. Finally, he got a sofa and a rug.

That should have sold it, but it didn't. So he went down with the price. Still, it did not sell.

Repackaging didn't work, so the next step was to *change the context*, which is meta-level repackaging. His ads, price and offer were targeting singles and families looking for an apartment. But what if it wasn't an apartment? What if he called it a club, a studio or a lounge? We changed the context from "living" to "partying". Selling it as a club, he could put the price up even higher than it was initially. People will pay more for something unique. In fact, "maybe you are not selling it because the price does not speak to a wealthier target group who would look for a club space," I told him.

But it was a residential area, so it was not possible to get a permit for a Bar or club. But it was possible to offer it to artists as a *studio,* a professional workspace overlooking the city.

That worked. The property sold to a photographer within weeks.

It may seem strange that raising a price makes a thing sell better, but people with extra money seek out the exclusive. A thing that is incomparable is difficult to sell otherwise. It's too weird, too quirky. But you can be sure that there is someone out there who will **fall in love** with that weird and quirky thing and be willing to pay *any price* for it. I am this way, and there are many others.

There is a metaphysical reason for this. The common, usual, normal and comparable comes from mind and Earth. The incomparable comes from Soul and Higher Realms. That's why it feels so **exciting**!

Some of my books are comparable to others on the topic. And some of my books, such as my most recent one (Extraterrestrial Linguistics), are incomparable–so much I can't even find their proper library category. My comparable books are usually ones that people demanded. The incomparable ones nobody asked for. The first kind is more difficult to write. The second kind is easier to write, because it comes from the Soul. It flows. The comparable book will be more successful, initially. The incomparable book may not sell much at first, but in the long run, it will be *legendary*. That's the difference between "mind based" and "soul based" work. Neither is "good" or "bad", they are just different experiences. The world needs both normal real estate, music, movies, books and restaurants that everyone can relate to, and it needs unique things that are unprecedented.

A special case (and flow-state) is achieved when you pursue a work that mixes mind and soul. The harmonizing of heaven and earth, soul and mind, mystical and practical, weird and common, creates more high energy and attraction than either of the two alone.

If you wish to attract your soulmate, you will need to live as your soul mate. And living as your soul means you become less predictable. What is it about you that is unlike any other?

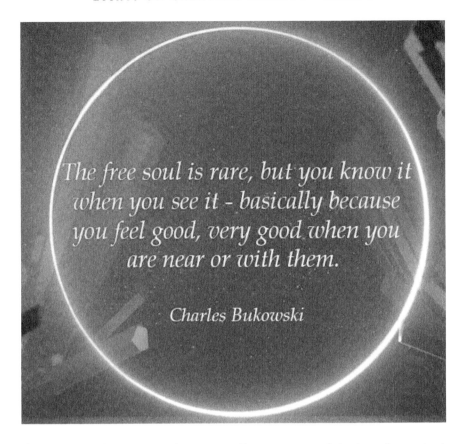

The free soul is rare, but you know it when you see it - basically because you feel good, very good when you are near or with them.

Charles Bukowski

If you wish to have a more business, allow it to sound, look and act a little different than similar businesses. I have coached a lot of coaches, and the thing that I had to advise on the most is that they sounded too much like a million other "life coaches" and needed to find their *niche* specialty before they could succeed. I mean… how many more people are going to call themselves "life coaches", for instance? Call yourself that, and you're only one of millions. What could you call yourself that *nobody else* calls themselves?

There is a Meditation I use to get in touch with the incomparable. It follows these simple instructions:

Put attention to a place you have never been, never seen, and have not yet imagined. Take your time to find it and daydream. Enjoy the sense of something beautiful, strange or alien.

You go to a place you have neither been in life, nor in your mind. Can you find such a place? Can you see, hear or feel something that is not based on a prior experience? It might be difficult at first, but with practice, you can become accustomed to thinking **way outside the box.** If you struggle to find something unique, then imagine going to a far away, inhabited planet.

Discovering the unfamiliar is akin to a horse escaping a carousel. A carousel keeps spinning the same old thoughts over and over. But you can awaken and <u>break out of the dull circles of life</u>, by thinking something you have never thought before.

22

Treat People Like They Are Healthy, Not Like They Are Sick

March 2021, exactly one year after Covid started and they told us it would be "over after two weeks of lockdown", was the first time I was denied entry into a shop because I did not sign in with a "contact-tracing app". The talk I had with the staffer was amusing:

"I don't have the tracing app,"

Staffer: *"Then you can't come in,"*

"If I don't own a phone, I can't shop here?"

Staffer (robotically): *"You need to sign in. Contact tracing."*

"But what about people who don't have a phone?"

Staffer: *"I see you're holding a phone,"*

"I'm perfectly healthy,"

Staffer: *"But you're gonna make others sick,"*

(I eventually signed in on paper).

By what kind of logic is my health going to make others sick? I have been healthy for the last 30 years, so why am I being treated as a sick person?

I have been perfectly healthy because of a strong immune system. The strong immune system comes from keeping my vibes up. If I give in to fear, I weaken my immune system. Isn't it common knowledge that treating people as sick makes them sick?

By forcing people to wear masks, go into quarantine when they travel and socially distancing, we make people act like they are sick when they are not. Acting sick is a psychiatric disorder called Munchhausen Syndrome. Look it up.

Predictably, governments now declare that free travel or even participation in public life will require a "vaccine passport". The same question applies: Why should I take a vaccine when I'm perfectly healthy?

"Uh, cuz you'll make others sick if you don't take it... duh ". Will I also make vaccinated people sick?

But how so? Aren't they promising protection for those who are vaccinated? So they have nothing to fear from me, who is not vaccinated, right? What's it to you whether I'm vaccinated? If I myself get vaccinated, how is it any of my business or concern whether others get vaccinated?

The law of most countries is that forced medication is illegal, with the exception of psychiatric prisons. By making vaccines mandatory for participation in public life, entire nations have descended to the level of psychiatric prisons with the inmates suffering from Munchausen syndrome.

I don't mind taking vaccines. I've taken many. Any negative side-effects of vaccines can easily be neutralized with good vibes. If I have to take it to travel, I will. But the coercive nature of this whole thing sets a negative precedent. Not allowing certain groups to participate in public life... remind you of anything in history?

The direction this whole thing is going: You will have an app which says whether you are "green lit" or "red lit" regarding your health. From that point forward, you will be a lifelong involuntary subscriber to the pharma industry and continually updated requirements for "variants" of viruses. Already now, shops and companies are being certified things for compliance with vaccine and covid regulations. You can tell this is the direction we are going, because scores of "celebrities" have been promoting certification by things like the "well building institute". First companies will require the wellness sticker, then individuals.

There is so much money being made with the fear-of-sickness industry that "social media" have quickly turned into censorship tools, banning hundreds of millions of users from openly discussing the subject. Entire groups discussing covid and vaccines are routinely banned. Videos and articles are covered with "fact checking" notices. In reality, Facebook or Twitter don't really give a damn about "fact checking" except when it comes to certain topics such as Covid or Vaccine. You could spend all day on Twitter denying that the middle ages happened or claiming that the post office is run by lizards or that AIDS doesn't exist. Nobody will put a fact-check sticker on that, because it's not part of the trillion-dollar covid and vaccine industry.

Treating people like they are sick is the worst attitude toward humans one can have. In a healthy society, only the sick are quarantined. Seeing everyone as a potential carrier of a contagious virus creates a general sense of mistrust and alienation. For a stronger immune system and better health, I recommend the exact opposite: **Meet people fearlessly.** Mingle. Exchange. Shake Hands. Touch. Breathe freely. Masks cut off oxygen intake. Lack of oxygen tends to lower IQ. The reason I have become immune to people who are not well is because I spent decades working with people who aren't well. You don't become strong by hiding.

I speak as someone who has been *perfectly healthy* for the last 30 years. Health comes from high energy, emotion, and consciousness. Your body, if unobstructed by fear-thoughts, regenerates itself.

The people running your Government struggle to accurately determine risk, predict outcomes and discern between what is and isn't healthy. Instead, they populate the Internet, secretly propagandizing for vaccines, as this coding accident using "gov" for Government reveals:

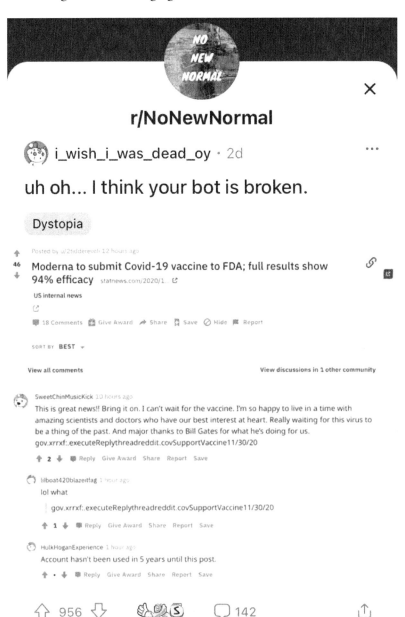

Yes, your elected officials employ Internet-bots to advertise vaccines.

And yes, sometimes they try to blackmail celebs into promoting vaccines. Just one example of several:

"I am opposed to vaccination and I wouldn't want to be forced by someone to take a vaccine in order to be able to travel". The statement came from #1 Ranking Tennis-Player Novak Djokovic. It's not enough that Djokovic was ripped apart by "the press". Soon, he was targeted for blackmail by organized crime. The Serbian model Natalija Scekic claims she was offered 60 000 Euros to entrap Djokovic, a married man with two children, with sex and make secret recordings of the event. The model declined and instead went to the press.

Obviously, they take their vaccine seriously. They restrict your freedom to work, freedom of movement and freedom of association in a desperate bid to get you to take the vaccine. I say bring on your damn vaccine already so we can have our life back. All of this pushing and propagandizing is unnecessary if you educate us and ask nicely. The *forcing* of it is what makes it suspicious.

As for the shop that denied my entry: After public backlash, local authorities ruled that the shop had to stop denying people entry. They had jumped the gun. Enough people stood up to it, so the shop was overruled. If nobody had stood up to it, nothing would have changed. Governments tend not to go back to normal. **You** need to go back to normal by standing your ground when it comes to unlawful mandates. Then they'll pretend they wanted to go back to normal all along.

Going back to normal means realizing that not social distancing but hugging people is good for your health. Meeting them offline is good for your health. Oxygen, not a mask, is good for your health. Travel is good for your health. Exposure to reality, not hiding from it, strengthens your immune system and is good for your health.

To be honest, the problem didn't just start with Covid. It was brewing long before that. When you visit a doctor, he or she would normally ask you about your diet, your sleep, your exercise, your water consumption, issues in the family, stress in your life, etc. Over time, it had become more and more profitable to ask less of these questions and instead prescribe pharmaceuticals. That's when we created an out-of-control pharmaceutical industry and a pill-addicted populace that was less healthy than ever. My wish is that from all of this, we create a world and populace, which takes back their health. I'm carefully optimistic that this could be the final result of it all.

23

Stages of Psychosocial Development

The following article is not mine, it is reproduced from here: The Stages of Psychosocial Development.

I have not reproduced the full article but extracted relevant parts of it. Even just a superficial awareness of these stages has helped me make sense of some of my students' experiences in my coaching work of the last 30 years. It's a fairly accurate model of different challenges one faces at different ages and how development might become arrested at a certain age.

If you are too rushed to read the whole article, you will also gain something by examining the two images below.

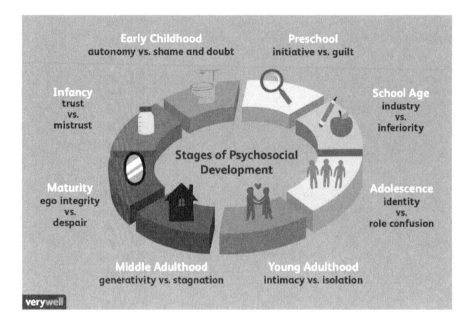

In summary: Trust, be autonomous, take initiative, work, know who you are, allow intimacy, create and integrate.

"Erik Erikson was an ego psychologist who developed one of the most popular and influential theories of development. Erikson's theory described the impact of social experience across the whole lifespan. Erikson was interested in how social interaction and relationships played a role in the development and growth of human beings.

Each stage in Erikson's theory builds on the preceding stages and paves the way for following periods of development. In each stage, Erikson believed people experience a conflict that serves as a turning point in development.

In Erikson's view, these conflicts are centered on either developing a psychological quality or failing to develop that quality. During these times, the potential for personal growth is high, but so is the potential for failure.

If people successfully deal with the conflict, they emerge from the stage with psychological strengths that will serve them well for the rest of their lives. If they fail to deal effectively with these conflicts, they may not develop the essential skills needed for a strong sense of self.

Erikson also believed that a sense of competence motivates behaviors and actions. Each stage in Erikson's theory is concerned with becoming competent in an area of life.

Stage 1: Trust vs. Mistrust

The first stage of Erikson's theory of psychosocial development occurs between birth and 1 year of age and is the most fundamental stage in life. Because an infant is utterly dependent, developing trust is based on the dependability and quality of the child's caregivers.

At this point in development, the child is utterly dependent upon adult caregivers for everything they need to survive, including food, love, warmth, safety, and nurturing. If a caregiver fails to provide adequate care and love, the child will come to feel that they cannot trust or depend upon the adults in their life.

If a child successfully develops trust, the child will feel safe and secure in the world. Caregivers who are inconsistent, emotionally unavailable, or rejecting contribute to feelings of mistrust in the children under their care. Failure to develop trust will result in fear and a belief that the world is inconsistent and unpredictable.

During the first stage of psychosocial development, children develop a sense of trust when caregivers provide reliability, care, and affection. A lack of this will lead to mistrust.

No child is going to develop a sense of 100% trust or 100% doubt. Erikson believed that successful development was all about striking a balance between the two opposing sides. When this happens, children acquire hope, which Erikson described as an openness to experience tempered by some wariness that danger may be present.

Stage 2: Autonomy vs. Shame and Doubt

The second stage of Erikson's theory of psychosocial development takes place during early childhood and is focused on children developing a greater sense of personal control.

At this point in development, children are just starting to gain a little independence. They are starting to perform basic actions on their own and making simple decisions about what they prefer. By allowing kids to make choices and gain control, parents and caregivers can help children develop a sense of autonomy.

The essential theme of this stage is that children need to develop a sense of personal control over physical skills and a sense of independence. Potty training plays an important role in helping children develop this sense of autonomy. Erikson believed that learning to control one's bodily functions leads to a feeling of control and a sense of independence. Other important events include gaining more control over food choices, toy preferences, and clothing selection.

Children who struggle and who are shamed for their accidents may be left without a sense of personal control. Success during this stage of psychosocial development leads to feelings of autonomy; failure results in feelings of shame and doubt.

Children who successfully complete this stage feel secure and confident, while those who do not are left with a sense of inadequacy and self-doubt. Erikson believed that achieving a balance between autonomy and shame and doubt would lead to will, which is the belief that children can act with intention, within reason and limits.

Psychosocial Stages: A Summary Chart

Age	Conflict	Important Events	Outcome
Infancy (birth to 18 months)	Trust vs. Mistrust	Feeding	Hope
Early Childhood (2 to 3 years)	Autonomy vs. Shame and Doubt	Toilet Training	Will
Preschool (3 to 5 years)	Initiative vs. Guilt	Exploration	Purpose
School Age (6 to 11 years)	Industry vs. Inferiority	School	Confidence
Adolescence (12 to 18 years)	Identity vs. Role Confusion	Social Relationships	Fidelity
Young Adulthood (19 to 40 years)	Intimacy vs. Isolation	Relationships	Love
Middle Adulthood (40 to 65 years)	Generativity vs. Stagnation	Work and Parenthood	Care
Maturity (65 to death)	Ego Integrity vs. Despair	Reflection on Life	Wisdom

Stage 3: Initiative vs. Guilt

The third stage of psychosocial development takes place during the preschool years. At this point in psychosocial development, children assert their power and control over the world through directing play and other social interactions.

Children who are successful at this stage feel capable and able to lead others. Those who fail to acquire these skills are left with a sense of guilt, self-doubt, and lack of initiative.

The major theme of the third stage of psychosocial development is that children need to begin asserting control and power over the environment. Success in this stage leads to a sense of purpose. Children who try to exert too much power experience disapproval, resulting in a sense of guilt.

When an ideal balance of individual initiative and a willingness to work with others is achieved, the ego quality, known as purpose, emerges.

Stage 4: Industry vs. Inferiority

The fourth psychosocial stage takes place during the early school years, from approximately ages 5 to 11. Through social interactions, children develop a sense of pride in their accomplishments and abilities.

Children need to cope with new social and academic demands. Success leads to a sense of competence, while failure results in feelings of inferiority.

Children who are encouraged and commended by parents and teachers develop a feeling of competence and belief in their skills. Those who receive little or no encouragement from parents, teachers, or peers will doubt their abilities to be successful.

Successfully finding a balance at this stage of psychosocial development leads to the strength known as competence, in which children develop a belief in their abilities to handle the tasks set before them.

Stage 5: Identity vs. Confusion

The fifth psychosocial stage takes place during the often turbulent teenage years. This stage plays an essential role in developing a sense of personal identity, which will continue to influence behavior and development for the rest of a person's life. Teens need to develop a sense of self and personal identity. Success leads to an ability to stay true to yourself, while failure leads to role confusion and a weak sense of self.

During adolescence, children explore their independence and develop a sense of self. Those who receive proper encouragement and reinforcement through personal exploration will emerge from this stage with a strong sense of self and feelings of independence and control. Those who remain unsure of their beliefs and desires will feel insecure and confused about themselves and the future.

When psychologists talk about identity, they are referring to all the beliefs, ideals, and values that help shape and guide a person's behavior. Completing this stage successfully leads to fidelity, which Erikson described as an ability to live by society's standards and expectations.

While Erikson believed that each stage of psychosocial development was important, he placed a particular emphasis on the development of ego identity. Ego identity is the conscious sense of self that we develop through social interaction and becomes a central focus during the identity versus confusion stage of psychosocial development.

According to Erikson, our ego identity constantly changes due to new experiences and information we acquire in our daily interactions with others. As we have new experiences, we also take on challenges that can help or hinder the development of identity.

Our personal identity gives each of us an integrated and cohesive sense of self that endures through our lives. Our sense of personal identity is shaped by our experiences and interactions with others, and it is this identity that helps guide our actions, beliefs, and behaviors as we age.

Stage 6: Intimacy vs. Isolation

Young adults need to form intimate, loving relationships with other people. Success leads to strong relationships, while failure results in loneliness and isolation. This stage covers the period of early adulthood when people are exploring personal relationships.

Erikson believed it was vital that people develop close, committed relationships with other people. Those who are successful at this step will form relationships that are enduring and secure.

Remember that each step builds on skills learned in previous steps. Erikson believed that a strong sense of personal identity was important for developing intimate relationships. Studies have demonstrated that those with a poor sense of self tend to have less committed relationships and are more likely to struggler with emotional isolation, loneliness, and depression.

Successful resolution of this stage results in the virtue known as love. It is marked by the ability to form lasting, meaningful relationships with other people.

Stage 7: Generativity vs. Stagnation

Adults need to create or nurture things that will outlast them, often by having children or creating a positive change that benefits other people. Success leads to feelings of usefulness and accomplishment, while failure results in shallow involvement in the world.

During adulthood, we continue to build our lives, focusing on our career and family. Those who are successful during this phase will feel that they are contributing to the world by being active in their home and community. Those who fail to attain this skill will feel unproductive and uninvolved in the world.

Care is the virtue achieved when this stage is handled successfully. Being proud of your accomplishments, watching your children grow into adults, and developing a sense of unity with your life partner are important accomplishments of this stage.

Stage 8: Integrity vs. Despair

The final psychosocial stage occurs during old age and is focused on reflecting on life. At this point in development, people look back on the events of their lives and determine if they are happy with the life that they lived or if they regret the things they did or didn't do.

Erikson's theory differed from many others because it addressed development throughout the entire lifespan, including old age. Older adults need to look back on life and feel a sense of fulfillment. Success at this stage leads to feelings of wisdom, while failure results in regret, bitterness, and despair.

At this stage, people reflect on the events of their lives and take stock. Those who look back on a life they feel was well-lived will feel satisfied and ready to face the end of their lives with a sense of peace. Those who look back and only feel regret will instead feel fearful that their lives will end without accomplishing the things they feel they should have..

Those who are unsuccessful during this stage will feel that their life has been wasted and may experience many regrets. The person will be left with feelings of bitterness and despair.

Those who feel proud of their accomplishments will feel a sense of integrity. Successfully completing this phase means looking back with few regrets and a general feeling of satisfaction. These individuals will attain wisdom, even when confronting death".

24

Will Extraterrestrial Contact Cause Mass Hysteria Or Mass Awakening?

There is a guy by the name of *Haim Eshed.* He says that some of our governments are working in an alliance with a "galactic federation of extraterrestrials" and their spaceships and that our leaders have been forbidden to tell the public because it would cause mass hysteria.

The seemingly far-out claim carries some weight because of who Haim Eshed is. His CV says that Eshed...

- was Colonel and Brigadier General in the *Military Intelligence Directorate* of Israel

- worked in the secretive *Unit 81,* which provided advanced technology to the IDF (Israeli Defense Force)

- is a professor of aeronautics and astronautics

- was the Director of Space Programs for the Ministry of Defense in Israel

- chaired the Space Committee at the Ministry of Science in Israel

- is credited with being the father of Israels' space program

- is responsible for the launch of 20 Israeli satellites

- is decorated with several of the highest awards of the country.

The reason I am listing these credentials is to make a point: None of these accomplishments protected him from being attacked as a *total madman* by our dumbed-down press.

From the link above:

"In December 2020, Eshed claimed in an interview with Israeli national newspaper Yediot Aharonot that the United States government had been in contact with extraterrestrial life for years and had signed secret agreements with a "Galactic Federation" in order to do experiments on Earth, and that there is a joint base underground on Mars where they collaborate with American astronauts".

There have been many people of rank and expertise, telling us similar stuff about galactic alliances, secret space programs, and beings in outer space. These sources usually also say that it would lead to "mass hysteria" and "hospitalize" people.

But would it? Really?

I don't think so.

Anyone reading this, having a breakdown? No? I didn't think so. Humans can handle a lot more than a couple of aliens.

Throughout History, many unexplained phenomena have been reported. *They lead to wonderment, not to mass hysteria.* Thousands of years of storytelling have prepared us for the possibility that something is "out there". In fact, we've already been visited many times. If we believe ancient scripture, beings from other worlds used to live *among us* thousands of years ago.

Whether spaceships are flying around above me or not, doesn't change that I take a shower in the morning, then get to work and maybe, a little later, have breakfast. Extraterrestrials are not such a big deal.

Why then, does it feel like mass awakening is feared, avoided and suppressed? Because it will tear us out of our cozy little world? But it won't. A spaceship flying to Mars has about as much impact on my life as an airplane crossing the Ocean.

Or is it that those spacefaring beings are so horrible, we couldn't handle it? I doubt it. Those who stay hidden are the ones more likely to be afraid. If they weren't afraid of us, they'd be out in the open. Perhaps they wish to remain secret so they can go about their business unobstructed.

The other day, a student of mine, who works in real estate, said this: *"I'm keeping all of my (house) listings secret. If I reveal them, they'll be stolen from me"*. I found that statement interesting. Keeping secrets ensures his survival. It's human nature to use secrecy to hoard power. The people keeping non-terrestrials their secret, then promote excuses such as "Those poor humans need to be protected from the psychological shock that disclosure would bring. ". That's not much different than saying: *"I didn't reveal that I was cheating on you, because I wanted to protect you from the hurt"*. But keeping the cheating a secret does not protect from the hurt, because the lie is felt subconsciously. We are all connected. We get paranoid because we sense "something is going on", but don't know what.

Ignorance isn't bliss. Even though truth can hurt a person initially, in the long run, it is always healing. If extra-terrestrials were revealed today, worldwide, it would bring humans closer together. Regardless of whether these non-terrestrials are benevolent.

According to my book Extraterrestrial Linguistics, however, something entirely different is going on. And I mean *completely different*. Aliens are us and we've always been interstellar travelers. Those UFOs you see in the sky are piloted by our cousins. We ourselves came from the stars. Planet Earth and the space around it, is a lower realm that causes amnesia of the higher realms we came from. So the real reason we don't know anything about these "Aliens" and "UFOs" is because of our own unawareness in this low-density realm. Hard to believe? Read my last two books!

25

Everything "Bad" That Happened To Me Was Good In The Long Run

If you are upset, you are only seeing a small scene of the movie, not the whole. The Universe is an apparatus of absolute genius and moves **everything to your best**. That's why all bad that has ever happened to me was for the good–in the long run. At first it didn't seem, look or sound good, but from a **sky-perspective,** every tragedy, drama, problem and challenge thrown my way was just what I needed to grow and be happier. Just a few examples:

- My car once broke down on the way to the airport. I missed my flight. The flight crashed, killing most passengers. I didn't get upset about the car breaking down, though. Why not? Because it happened at a time in my life, when I already knew that everything happens to our favor. **There is a good reason things happen.**

- At age 26, I had my first "heartbreak", when my girlfriend left me. At the time, I thought it was the *worst* thing that could happen and that the good life was over. Today, I realize just how lucky I am that she left me. Had I stayed with her, I wouldn't have met my soulmate. I would be with a woman who, in retrospect, is not my type in *any* way. How delusional we are to assume that the things happening to us are "bad".

- Once, *all* the money I had made and saved up through life had been stolen from me. I had to start all over. At the time, I thought that was really unfair and "bad". Today I realize it liberated me from dependence on money. I remembered that the goal was never money, it was spending the day as I wish, with who I wish and speaking my mind freely. That's what it was about!

I learned a new word the other day–Pronoia. That's the belief that the world is secretly conspiring in your favor. It's the opposite of Paranoia. That's my new favorite word, because it's exactly how I feel.

People think that 2020 was the "worst" year ever, because of all the lockdowns and the threat of a virus. But I see it as one of the BEST years ever, because more people than EVER are finally asking the right questions about Government, Civil Rights, Freedom, Community and Health. Have there ever been this many people researching, debating, learning about the world we live in? Sometimes it takes a crisis to awaken.

When something "bad" happens to you, it's the Universe saying "wait and see, before you get upset. Wait and see".

Based on all this, did you know there is a way to reduce the occurrence of "negative events"? Yes, you can influence your reality.

How? Well, looking back at your life, you'll notice that the "negative" events were there to teach you a lesson and correct your course. So if you do not want "bad" things to happen, then don't require correction. Relax so that you can listen to your heart. Follow your heart (the gentle inner voice that tells you right from wrong, authentic from fake, really you from posing) and you'll be on the right path. Then Life won't have to make up tragedy and drama to remind you of following your heart.

26

Think for Yourself

The first step to higher consciousness is to think for yourself. The second step is to think big. And the final step is to let go of thinking and allow intuition to guide you. Let's take the first step together. It has not yet been taken by most.

Your thoughts, mental images, opinions, beliefs and ideas: *Are they yours?*

Can you imagine, for a moment, a pink elephant floating in the sky?

That's how easy it is to provide a thought for you to think. It's not yours–I put it there. I implanted it in your mind. You did not consciously choose or create it. This is the norm. Most of your thoughts were put there by others. You have tens of thousands of thoughts each week of which you probably didn't say:

"I like this thought. I choose to make it my own."

Some of the thoughts people give you are well-intended, some aren't. But even well-intended thoughts are not always true.

If you have TV or radio running, it happens thousands of times a day. An image on the TV screen or in a Smartphone, is a thought, no different than those of the mind. Many indiscriminately buy into whatever is presented on screen. Scroll through Instagram or TikTok and you can feed yourself a hundred thoughts in five minutes. People use it to drown out what they really feel. Even though you consciously claim not to buy into the images fed to you, the subconscious is influenced.

To awaken fully, that needs to stop. I got rid of my TV 30 years ago, but if I still had one, the least I'd do is to *carefully choose* the programs I watch. The word "program" itself doesn't mask what TV is: programming. If you're going to use "entertainment", then at least choose what you program yourself with.

So are your thoughts yours? Most of them aren't. The naïve, untrained mind takes its thoughts from others. And if there are no others, it takes its opinions from the great thought-generators called TV, radio and Internet.

Our first exercise in thinking for yourself: In a few seconds, I am again going to ask you to imagine a pink elephant floating in the sky. But instead of imagining what I tell you, I'd like you to imagine *something of your choosing*. Let's try.

Can you imagine, for a moment, a pink elephant floating in the sky?

If you *defied* my instruction by choosing your own thought, you've successfully completed the exercise.

That was easy, right? But only because you consciously intended to defy the thought I provided. Wouldn't it be hard to monitor every single thought that comes my way? It would. And I don't recommend it, because it's too difficult to sustain long term. All I am suggesting is to take some time in a week, to be more discerning between thoughts that are genuinely yours and those that aren't.

Believe it or not, most people are conditioned to such a degree that they have difficulty defying external commands. They'll say "I tried, but it was hard not seeing that pink elephant!". Just because it was easy for you, don't assume it is for others.

I could have said "think nothing", but it's easier to defy external impositions by pivoting to *something else*–a beautiful landscape, a car, a house, making love–the more intense the thing pictured, the easier it is to keep attention.

Let's do another exercise.

Do not think of a pink elephant in the sky now. I repeat, do not think of the Pink Elephant. And don't think of an orange car either. Do not think of the orange car!

What happened? The command *not* to think of something is almost the same as the command to think of it. Those untrained in thinking for themselves will have thought of an orange car when I told them not to, even if briefly. Some thought they are *defying* my command by thinking of an orange car! But a person (or media outlet) that is telling you *not* to think something is subconsciously (or secretly) telling you to think of it.

The subconscious doesn't process the "don't" or "not". If we were walking in a crowd, and I say about one woman "Don't look at her", I am putting your attention on her. If I didn't want you to notice her, it would be best I say nothing. This is why what we resist will persist and why "negative publicity is also publicity".

If most thoughts are not yours, how can I tell which thoughts are mine? Well, let's do an exercise:

Write 5 thoughts you'd like to have.

Was that easy to do? How did it feel to choose your own thoughts? Self-chosen thoughts feel better than imposed thoughts.

Example: *I choose to think that this article awakens something deep and profound in you that changes the trajectory of your life.*

I chose that thought, and there is nothing anyone can do about that.

How much power does that thought have to affect my reality? That depends upon how many contradicting thoughts get in its way. When I formed that thought, it stood unopposed. I imagined it clear as day and felt a warmth in my chest radiating into the world. Choosing the thought affected me positively and is likely to affect some of my readers.

In an untrained mind, the self-chosen positive thought will likely trigger internal objections. For example:

"I don't know if this article will have that affect. Maybe it's boring"

"It's not up to me to know"

"This sucks, I want to do something else"

"Really? I doubt it."

If these doubts were to arise, then I either need to a) write a better article or b) create a more realistic thought or c) release my doubts and practice my new thought.

The word "doubt" derives from the Latin word for "two". It means that attention is split between two things. A sense of certainty or belief comes from being able to think about one thing, unobstructed by doubts.

I could write a better article and that would soothe my doubts. Or I could create a more realistic self-chosen positive thought, such as *"It is my wish that this article help people feel better"*. That could be more believable than *"This article awakens something deep and profound that changes the trajectory of your life"*. I recommend not to think too small or too big. Thinking too small doesn't the needle of emotion. Thinking too big can become overwhelming, putting the frequencies you are aiming for out of reach. If you are struggling financially, thinking "I am a billionaire" is probably not in your reach and holding that thought won't have any effect on your inner state. But thinking "I will get any random job, just to get by" doesn't feel inspiring either. There must be something in between the very high and low thought? How about this: *"I do what it takes to find a product, service or value I can provide to the world and make good money with".* Doesn't that resonate more than those two other thoughts?

Or I could consciously practice to release unwanted thoughts and re-align with preferred thoughts. That's an exercise I'll leave you with as homework. The technique is useful and universal. It can be used by anyone at any time.

1. Make a list of five thoughts you've been having that you'd prefer not to have.

2. Now list five thoughts of your own choosing that you'd like to have instead. Make them realistic but positive, neither too low nor too high.

3. Intentionally create (think) the negative thought. Then intentionally create (think) the positive thought. Hold each for 10 to 60 seconds.

4. Now intentionally think each positive thought on the list.

The reason you intentionally think negative thoughts is to bring them under conscious control. They used arise automatically, now they arise intentionally. Then you show the subconscious what you'd like to think instead. When you show yourself the negative and positive side by side, the subconscious, automatically and naturally begins working in the direction of the positive. This is because the subconscious job is to assist in your survival and well-being.

I recommend this as a weekly practice, over several months. Every week you look at your thought list and take stock: Which old thoughts have disappeared, which are still there? Update your list accordingly and repeat the exercise. If you do this week by week, you will find that foreign thoughts fade and your self-chosen thoughts become more dominant. As a result, your health, finances and relationships improve.

These are mere baby steps in thinking for yourself. The long-term implications are profound. You gradually de-condition yourself from the world-mind and think a few octaves more creatively and optimistically than the majority of people. Your insights become fresh and unique, unlike the repetitive and stale propaganda of "conventional" schooling, media, corporate and state lingo. This is the "think big" phase mentioned above. Thoughts feel exciting because they come from a higher cosmic intelligence, from the soul level. The final phase is to be guided more by intuition than by thought. Here, the mind is mostly serene. No inner chatter. Decisions and actions arise from the moment, based on what feels right. Past indoctrination is not required to handle the situation in the present. Life is lived in a state of flow, more effortlessly than the grasping gripping, over-focused mind.

And it all starts with a basic awareness of a) your most dominant thoughts and b) the thoughts you'd like to choose instead. This is how you think for yourself.

27

Social Media Is A Bit Of A Scam

Articles like these usually sit on my website for months before I publish them. I don't want to publish them, because I wish to spread good news. On the other hand, it's my responsibility to inform my fellow humans truthfully.

You see–Social Media is useful for many things, but there's also a shadow-side.

1. Hidden Censorship

Over the years I have had many people ask me why they can't see my posts, even though they follow me. The question comes up so often, it's *tiresome.*

This comment was received just today:

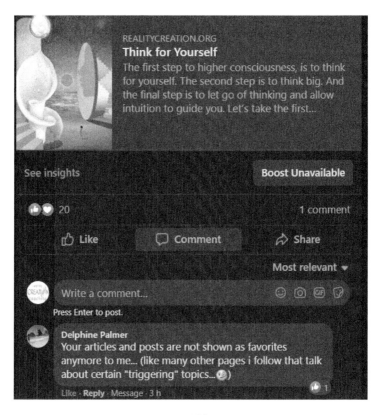

Yes… these companies really are that creepy. They *really* do sit there and edit peoples reach, without disclosing the fact and without sharing reasons.

Open censorship, as in Terms and Conditions, I don't mind. But secretly hiding pages and accounts, even though they don't violate their terms? Pretty crazy if you ask me!

Just moving this into my non-fiction section…

Remember telephoning pre-Internet? Now imagine the phone company editing your talk or blocking the line because they don't like what you said to your friend. Sound weird? It's what Instagram recently, when they put a warning label on top of them so that they could not be seeing without first clicking and looking at the "fact checkers". That's why, a few days ago, I deleted my Instagram account and the 3000 posts on it (in case you were wondering where it disappeared to).

Do companies that engage in hidden censorship have a future? I doubt it. I've already quit using these companies privately, because they sell my data. I only use them to spread to share my work, for that they are useful.

2. There is no Organic Reach

Since a whole decade, Facebook, Twitter and similar, show me stats that stay pretty much the same, no matter how many or how few people read an article of mine. On my website I can see the *actual* statistics of how many read a post. But a *strong decrease* in numbers (because my website is temporarily down) or a *strong increase* in numbers, sometimes in the tens of thousands, has no bearing on my social media "stats".

Sometimes an "influencer" or celebrity mentions one of my books. Those are the times my website is overwhelmed with traffic, often taking it offline for a few hours, as we scramble to get it back up. **These surges in traffic cannot be seen on my social media accounts.** If some "influencer" with Millions of followers, mentions me, my website might temporarily go up from 8000 to 40 000 visitors in a day. But on places like Twitter it's still the exactly same amount of views and likes and has been so with very little change for the last 10 years. Just like 10 Years ago, I get an average of 4 to 6 likes on articles I post to Twitter. No change whatsoever.

Reality Creation @RealityCreation · 20h

realitycreation.org/think-for-your... #lawofattraction #realitycreation #selfdetermination

Think for Yourself
The first step to higher consciousness, is to think for yourself. The second step is to think big. And the final step is to let go of thinking a...
🔗 realitycreation.org

Weird, huh? Talk about content suppression! Contrast the average of 4 to 6 people liking a post of mine on Twitter, to my average Youtube stats:

My video channel receives around 20 000 views a month. My Twitter account receives around 500 views a month. How can that be reconciled? It can't, unless Twitter is *actively manipulating* the numbers or suppressing content.

Even though the Youtube numbers are much higher, I don't trust those numbers either! On my website, it only takes me a couple of days to reach 40 000, on Youtube it supposedly takes me two months. Most of my Videos have an average of 4000 views. But sometimes there is a crack in the Matrix and a *radically* different number is shown, as on these Videos:

Types of Angels, Aliens and Entities

60,464 views · Apr 10, 2018 👍 LIKE 👎

Frederick Dodson

Raising Your Frequency

81,908 views • Jan 15, 2014   👍 LIKE 👎 |

Frederick Dodson

If most of my Videos have an average of "4000 views", how is it possible that beside those, there are Videos with 81 000 and 60 000 views? If that many people viewed these Videos, at least *some* would have also viewed others. By logic, the discrepancy of 81 000 or even 60 000 to an average of 3000 to 4000 views, is too high. If 80 000 is the max, then you'd expect 50 000 to be the minimum. And if 4000 is the minimum, you'd expect the maximum to be around 7000. *The numbers don't make sense and point to some type of mistake or manipulation.* Did someone forget to throttle the numbers on those Videos, or is it just an innocent technical error? But now those numbers, as high as they are, have been nearly unchanging for several years, which is also improbable.

Fortunately I don't rely on social media, as 99% of my coaching-students come from word-of-mouth recommendation and do not know me through social media (in fact, many of my regular students didn't even know I write articles and books when they booked me!)

Why would social media companies go out of their way to throttle or suppress content?

Because allowing ideas to spread organically, like in the early days of Internet, is "dangerous", apparently. Both Twitter and Facebook gave up "organic reach" years ago.

ORGANIC FACEBOOK REACH IN APAC
2015-2018

bonsey

5.4%

2.8%

2.4%

1.2%

2015   2016   2017   2018

Source

Information is more controlled than ever. There is a school of thought among Governments, that is worried of giving common people large spheres of influence. As if we aren't smart and mature enough to have organic reach or to choose what we'd like to see.

Not only that, they actively monitor every little thing posted. Take this recent article on Yahoo News for example:

U.S. Postal Service is running a covert operations program that monitors peoples social media posts.

"The law enforcement arm of the U.S. Postal Service has been quietly running a program that tracks and collects Americans' social media posts, including those about planned protests, according to a document obtained by Yahoo News. The details of the surveillance effort, known as iCOP, or Internet Covert Operations Program, have not previously been made public".

But would genuine terrorists openly post their plans on social media? Or are they just looking for excuses to monitor everyone?

3. Numbers can be manipulated

I'm skeptical of the numbers thrown around. I've worked with people who have hundreds of thousands or even millions of "followers" on social media… and yet… in our Coaching session, they admit they are struggling to earn a living. How does that fit together? I once had a student who had 3 Million (!) followers, but struggled to pay my $399 Coaching Fee (back then), asking if he could split the payment in 4 parts. I declined, so he had to save up for a few months. I asked him, but he evaded the question, claiming that his 3 Million followers "don't necessarily translate into Business". But I don't believe that. I think either he purchased his followers or someone fixed the numbers for him. I told him that.

Conclusion

No matter from which angle you look at it, social media is a bit of a scam. So why don't I migrate to "alternative" social media? Because I don't trust those either. I do have active accounts on <u>MeWe</u> and <u>Minds</u> though. If I ever disappear from Facebook and Twitter, you'll find me on one of the many alternatives.

Disclaimer: I don't need any helpful comments on what I need to "succeed" on social media. I quit seeking that kind of "success" long ago. I am happy with things in my life as they are.

28

What You See In Others
Is Within Yourself

This is an exercise to show how the world is a reflection of you. We sometimes see the world not as it is, but as we are. To see people as they really are, reduce your opinions and projections and look with fresh eyes, unobstructed by past events. A hint: If you feel compassion or appreciation, you are closer to seeing people as they really are and less into projecting.

Step 1: Write the names of a few people you like or are attracted to.

Step 2: Write what qualities make these people likable or attractive.

Step 3: Write how these traits remind you of qualities within yourself.

Step 4: Write the names of a few people you dislike or are not attracted to.

Step 5: Write the qualities that make these people unlikable or unattractive.

Step 6: Write how these traits remind you of qualities within yourself.

These are the easy steps, but if you wish to take this exercise into an even deeper experience, continue with the following:

Step 7: Have others in your circle of friends or family do the same exercise so that you can compare your projections to theirs.

Step 8: Tell a few people what you like about them and how these items remind you of things within yourself.

Step 9: Tell a few people what you dislike about them and how these items remind you of things within yourself.

Step 10: Write what you learned about yourself and your beliefs. Examine whether you were honest and if not, what kept you from being entirely honest.

If you stay open to it, you may learn some surprising things both about yourself and why you have attracted certain people into your life and business. Both the things you resist and the things you appreciate, you attract into your life.

(Note to Seminar-Facilitators: This exercise is powerful in group-training scenarios of more than 10 people. Yes, it takes some courage to conduct it).

29

Releasing Food Addiction through Intermittent Fasting

Intermittent fasting means to put aside a regular time in the day, when you do not eat. For example, I do not eat between 6 pm in the evening and 11 am the next day. This gives my stomach 17 hours to digest, clear out and rest. I have been practicing this for the last three years. Not fanatically–sometimes I break the rule. "Everything in moderation, including moderation". It was easy for me to make this a habit, because I never enjoyed eating in the morning, anyway. I had been conditioned, in childhood, to believe that I "need" breakfast to be healthy, even though I was never hungry in the morning.

Intermittent fasting provides an extra boost of energy. And I am all about energy!

Contrary to popular belief, over-indulgence does not provide energy. Eating for sustenance provides some energy, but if you go beyond that it depletes energy. Food addiction is common. Many "foods" are unethically made to be addictive to increase sales. Ask yourself:

If there is a "health foods" section in the supermarket, then what is the rest of the food?

The good news is that our body will cleanse itself if we give it a chance to. If we stuff it non-stop with foods at every hour, it does not have a chance to cleanse itself. But with intermittent fasting, it's like you get a brand new, lighter, healthier body every day.

If you wish to know whether you are food addicted, check: Can you go a day without food? If not, you're addicted. Can you at least go 12 hours without food? If not, you are extremely addicted.

I am not suggesting that my way of fasting must be good for anyone. But I am suggesting that you reduce your dependence on foods. More important than "which diet" to take, is the ability to do without food for certain times. There are a number of other ways that energy can be taken in, such as breathing, high-level-thought, releasing heavy emotions, love and creative work. It doesn't always have to be food. Your energy-state is partially regulated by the kinds of foods you eat and how much you eat. When you are food-addicted, it could feel as if eating a less depletes your energy. But it's not the less eating that depletes it, it's the mental addiction. And the best way to overcome the addiction is to set aside certain times where you don't eat and stick to it for some time. My 17 hours may be too extreme for you. In this case, you might start with something easier, such as 8 pm to 10 am, which is 14 hours of rest, so that your body can do its job.

I have seen some people heal various health conditions with intermittent fasting. Rather than adding to their intake with medication, they lessened their intake through fasting. Regardless of what health condition you are dealing with, intermittent fasting should be one of the things you try on your path to recovery.

You will notice just how habitual eating is for most people and that it's rarely out of hunger and mostly out of pleasure. Beyond a certain point, it's no longer pleasure. Then it turns into the burden of craving. You become aware that it's this way with other things in life too. When you temporarily remove the thing you are addicted to, it exposes the emotions that were masked by the continual "pleasure-seeking". In the absence of the habitual meal, you get a chance to feel and release those emotions. And behind that, you find out who you really are. And you become even more well.

30

Atheists are Secret Believers

Atheists are Believers, they just don't know it. And religious fanatics struggle with their belief, but may not know it. I realize that writing this might offend, but someone has to say it.

Where you find one side of a polarity to the *extreme*, you find the other. Usually the other side of the polarity is subconscious.

Atheists of the militant kind, think about God all the time. They think about God more than religious people. You find them online posting about God, from the opposing side. God and Religion live rent-free in their head. They are intensely curious about Religion, Religious People, Religious Life, continually observing, commenting and critiquing. If you truly don't believe something, then you don't make much mention of it.

I'd even go so far as to say, they love their Creator so very much, they deny their Creators existence. Sound nonsensical? Consider this: If you rabidly, crazily love a person, but that person does not give you any attention, what do you do? Normally, the mind goes to the opposite pole and denies that persons' existence. Deep down, atheists feel they are not getting the attention of their Creator. They claim not to believe in God, but are the ones who think about God all the time. Atheists are also keenly focused on truth-finding ("show me the evidence!"), just like their religious counterparts.

Religious Fanatics—those obsessed with Religion, taking it extremely seriously, set to convince and convert others by force—secretly doubt their Creator. Again.... does that sound nonsensical? Then consider this:

If they really believed in their Creator, they wouldn't have to keep forcing the issue. If you have trust and confidence in something, there is no need to convince others. **Confidence is calm, insecurities are loud.** Excessive zeal means that the person, deep down, doesn't really believe. The religious fanatic is subconsciously an atheist. And the atheist is subconsciously a religious fanatic. That's why religious fanatics make Religion look bad. If they were true believers, they'd be representing their Religion in a more attractive way.

As offensive as this seems, the mind does work on polarity and this principle applies to many other things too. People who are fervently committed to hating on homosexuals, might be subconsciously attracted to them or have some other issue with sexuality. Those who see racism everywhere and define everything from the lens of "race", may have been victimized based on race, and therefore subconsciously become racist themselves. Yes, again, I realize how controversial that sounds and that some readers would rather attack me for saying these things than confront subconscious shadows, but that's alright. My job, in 35 years of Coaching, has been to confront peoples subconscious shadow. And usually, when a person attacks me for it, it means they are subconsciously considering it. The point is: Where you see a total fanatic to one side, the other side is also present, subconsciously.

The two sides of a polarity are one unit. There is Mountain Peak and Valley, but both are part of the same unit called Mountain. There is no up without down, no left without right, no hot without cold. Cold can only be known in comparison to hot. Relaxation is known because before that, there was the opposite: Tension. Tension is known because of Relaxation. Things are created whole, but we divide them into duality. Hot and Cold are both part of the same topic: Temperature. Belief in God and Atheism are both part of the same topic: Faith.

People who go from one extreme to another, as in a Pendulum, show an imbalance, that requires addressing (if that person wishes to feel better). In a balanced state, there is some debate, then there is choice. That's why, where you find a fanatic, you often find earlier abuse. It's not uncommon for a fanatic (whatever they are fanatic about), to have been abused, mistreated or betrayed by people of the opposite belief.

That's why I agree with this statement: "Everything in Moderation. Including Moderation". When I see myself getting too preoccupied with one side of a thing, I intentionally start exploring the other side of it, just to find a well-rounded balance. That doesn't mean I see everything neutrally and don't take in any position. I take many clear positions on a number of things, but because I trust in them, there is no need to broadcast them in a pushy or fanatic manner. If a person questions my work, there is no need to put that person down or defend myself. That's true belief vs. shaky belief, confidence vs. fanaticism. True belief creates your reality.

Is there anything beyond polarity? In my view, the Absolute is beyond polarity. Love and Source are beyond polarity.

31

A Vaccine Against Fear

In the last weeks, I've received around thirty emails from people, asking me if they should take the vaccine.

But I'm *the wrong person to ask,* as I have about as much medical expertise as Bill Gates–none at all.

Even so, this article is a reply to all the emails, from my personal perspective:

More important than whether you will take the vaccine is whether you live in fear or courage.

Those who use fear to manipulate people into pre-determined choices like to provide "two sides" to give the Illusion of choice. Both sides are fear-based. In this case, the two "sides" are pro-vaxxers and anti-vaxxers. Supposed "Anti-vaxxers" put out fear-information about people dying from taking the vaccine, getting horrible sores, becoming sterilized, how they put nanotechnology into vaccines, how it has tracking devices in it. Most of these "conspiracy theories" aren't true, they are just put out there to obscure *real* conspiracies (such as financial ties between vaccine companies, labs in Wuhan and profiteering politicians). Do some people die? Sure. Just like some people die off of Covid or some people die by slipping on a banana peel or driving their car down the road. But just like with Covid, most people don't experience any adverse effects at all.

On the "other side" we have the Covid-Cult, who treat everyone as sick until proven healthy. Around the world, they preach their daily sermon of fear through what we now understand to be tightly controlled media-outlets. If this were a real pandemic, you'd be seeing dead animals and homeless people lying around. You wouldn't have gift shops selling covid fashion. Custom Inspection would not only find traces of cocaine on money, they'd find actual traces of Covid. And places that didn't have lockdowns would be worse off than places that did. But that's not the case. The whole thing is a fear-racket. That's why it has to be repeated every day.

Why don't we get this many alerts and reminders about Tuberculosis? 10 Million people contracted it last year and a staggering 1.5. Million people died of it. What about Heart Disease or Cancer, which are much greater causes of death than Covid? Why aren't they not even getting a tiny fraction of the Budget and attention that "Covid" is getting?

Because the ruling elite is urgently peddling something, to get a large number of people to act by using fear and repetition. The goal is a global health validation system, which will eventually turn into a global ID system and finally into a global social credit system.

The problem with that plan is that many people don't fear, so the plan isn't going to work unless they unleash a *real* pandemic. Does that thought scare you? Well, it shouldn't, because fear is what would *attract* such a mass-scenario. Fear, in and of itself, is a greater risk than any virus, any vaccination and any politician.

Is there a vaccine against Fear? Fear is the real virus. And the cure is Love.

Some people are afraid of not taking the vaccine, some are afraid of taking it. My only advice is: Stop being afraid.

If you're afraid, it means you don't know how powerful your soul is. A healthy soul-body-mind can easily handle both virus and vaccine.

So am I going to take it? Not right now, maybe later. I'll watch you take it first. Not that I mind vaccines, but I do mind the authoritarian bullying, as in "if you don't take the vaccine, you will never travel again".

What is the best thought to have about the virus and vaccine? It is that you will be just fine with or without it. That belief puts your body to rest. When your body is no longer tense, the immune system works better and you are overall healthier. The person writing here hasn't been sick or unwell in more than 30 years. That's because I believe in fearlessness, hugs, courage and socially connecting–the exact opposite of the programming.

To be honest, I can't even remember when I was last at the doctor. But I've already received 5 unsolicited alerts on my phone to go get a vaccine. I was listening to a podcast on my Amazon app the other day, but it kept getting interrupted by an ad for me to get a vaccine. That kind of repetitive propaganda bothers me, because it's how you train robots and animals–through constant repetition they didn't ask for. This kind of "advertising" unfortunately works, but it only works with people who haven't awakened their spiritual-self. The spiritual-self is immune to repetition-drills, it is guided by Intuition.

In fact, a much greater problem than Covid or Vaccines is the method and manner in which politics, large corporations and media work together to blast an internationally unified message into mass -consciousness, getting the majority to act. Their ability to use fear and misinformation to get the majority to take action is too much power in the hands of a few. Today they can spread their fear-virus on the topic of Covid–how are they going to use this power tomorrow?

The best thought to have about this is the idea that we, as individuals, can start taking back our life at a local level and develop a healthy skepticism and boycott mass-propaganda. Boycotting companies that use fear-based programming lies in your power and has real-world consequences.

32

The World Is A Mirror

I recently talked to someone who moved out of town. He moved away because horrible things happened to him in this town. He got beaten up by Gang-members in broad daylight. Another time, he got assaulted by a stranger for no reason. On another occasion, he was attacked and bitten by a dog, apparently while sitting in his car with the window rolled down. What a horrible town! So he moved to what he believed was a better place.

Can you guess what happened to him at the better place? In his first week there, his car and laptop were stolen.

I live in the same town he moved away from. I have never been assaulted, beaten, or bitten. Nothing was ever stolen from me. My experience in this town has been nothing but beautiful. I have met a lot of kind and smart people. I have enjoyed some of the most beautiful landscapes and climate this planet has to offer. I have been super creative-productive. It has been all peace for years. What a beautiful place!

It's easy to see that the world mirrors each person. It's easier to see in other people than oneself. But others can easily see it in you. They understand why you attract certain good or bad events into your life. You are talking about what is happening in your life, and they internally "get" why that is happening to you.

You can enhance your experience of life by a more intimate awareness of this: your external reality is a reflection of your inner reality. Everyone that crosses your path, every encounter, everything that happens to you, is there for a reason as a response to your inner state. Life is a love letter that your Higher Self is sending you every day. All "good" and "bad" things are there to help you learn and grow. Even the "bad" things are sent with love to help you grow stronger.

Sometimes "the Universe" sends you a message through another person. Once you understand the message, the person disappears or the message stops. Some problems repeat until you understand their message. They are there for you to learn and grow. You are never sent bigger problems than you can handle. Some problems are wake-up calls. If you want a problem-free life, stay awake and aware. As soon as you change, your surroundings and external reality either appear differently than before or change entirely.

Appreciate the little things that cross your path on a daily basis. "To appreciate" means to know they are there for a reason, that there are no coincidences, that everything has meaning. Nothing in your surroundings is happening independent of your own energy and identity. Even if you are not sure how it reflects your inner-self, acknowledge that it does. This is how to go from victim-consciousness of "the world happens to me" to the creator-consciousness of "the world happens through me".

33

Acting Like A Millionaire
Costs You $0

To more rapidly achieve your goal, act as if you already have it. It's the **"acting-as-if"** method of manifesting a reality (see my book <u>Reality Creation and Manifestation</u> for details).

People with financial goals have taken this to mean they should spend like a Millionaire, even though they aren't. *"But if I'm acting as if I'm a Millionaire, I'd be spending a lot more money,"* they tell me. But would you really? Most Millionaires, I know, are more into MAKING money than spending it. *Unconscious consumerism* is more a trait of the poor than the rich.

Acting Rich is Having Character

It costs $0 to act-like-a-Millionaire. None of the traits that lead to financial success actually cost any money. This is a list of things that will make you successful, that don't cost any money:

Service

Integrity

Creativity

Ethics

Respect

Love

Common Sense

Patience

Enthusiasm

Trust

Love

It costs you nothing to practice any of these. The only way to get rich *cleanly* (no strings attached*)*, is through these character-traits. The value of your enthusiasm for your work is immeasurable.

A lot of people tell me that before they can "get rich", they need to invest loads of money, but that kind of thinking is circular. It's true that you can get even richer if you are already rich. But if you are not rich, you don't have money to invest. Instead, you can be rich within (see the list of traits above). *It's predictable that these traits in Business, eventually turn into real riches.* The real purpose of business is, in fact, to bring people together so that they can practice these traits. As such, business is a good and spiritual activity. Seeing it that way will help your financial state. Most people see business as something non-spiritual or even ethically questionable. Thinking that way sabotages your own abundance. There is nothing more ethical than an exchange of value that makes both sides of the exchange more trusting, reliable, creative, etc.

Acting Rich is Having Something to Offer

Back when I still read LinkedIn messages, I'd receive one like this every other day:

"Hi Fred, I am reaching out to you to explore opportunities to help you get a six-figure income as a Coach ".

I once responded: A six-figure income would be a step backwards!

I receive hundreds (!) "notifications" a day, across different platforms. Many expect some kind of response, while giving or offering…

nothing.

Consider the message above. Whoever sent me that, doesn't bother finding out who they are talking to or what my needs might be.

An email I got the other day: "Hey, I know Rick, who once did a Podcast with you. I'd like to meet you personally to talk about a few things that have been bothering me." I declined, so he got more pushy: "I'm a friend of Ricks!" as if that meant that I owe him something.

Some people do offer me stuff, but don't bother finding out whether I am at all interested in what they are offering. Believe it or not, several times a year, I receive offers for sex. Where were all these offers when I was 20 years old? I'd have loved them back then! Today, I have zero interest. I am offered consultation, tarot-card laying, astrology consultations, advice for my writing, advice on which topics I'm supposed to write and thousands of other things I never asked for.

Offering people stuff they don't ask for, is a poor Business Model. Great customer-service is to find out what your customer wants, and offer that.

Only Businesses that do **what customers like** thrive. Any exception to this rule hints at corruption.

So what do I want that you could offer me? Nothing, frankly. LOL. I'm happy. If I ever need anything, I'll let you know! But honestly, intuitive people prefer looking for stuff themselves.

The basis of effective marketing is to know what the other person wants and to offer that. It is marketing that addresses a persons higher self, not the repetitive-brainwashing-marketing that addresses the lower-self.

The problem with most marketing is that it's founded on false and outmoded ideas that don't work on people of average intelligence. Propaganda, repetition and coercion only work on the weak-minded. Fortunately, more and more people are getting fed up with fear-based and conditioning-based ways.

Acting Rich is Being Authentic

Some people ask why I am not smiling in many of my photos. The reason is, I don't like smiling on command, because it's not a real smile. A real smile is when **I'm being photographed while having fun and don't even know I am being photographed**. You know how few selfies people post on their Instagram are spontaneous? Very few. But spontaneous photos (photos taken unprepared, without you knowing) always have more authentic energy to them. Sure, I post a lot of photos where I am "posing", but at least I am not trying to convey emotions I don't feel in that very moment. I recall meditating on a mountain top. Every couple of minutes, some tourists would reach the mountain top in a normal mood. Then they would briefly act ecstatic while taking selfies and then return to their regular mood. It was a hilarious display of inauthenticity. I'm not judging it. I'm just saying that inauthentic ecstasy makes it more difficult to experience real ecstasy. Being in touch with how you really feel makes it much easier to change how you really feel.

For the same reason, I don't write as good when writing at request, than writing from inspiration. Non-robotic, higher-self people, are better with self-chosen tasks than with ones imposed.

Fake Smiles are very common. Advertisement and Model Photography are full of fake smiles. Good photographers get their models to find real joy. A good movie director will do numerous takes of a scene if the actress is not feeling the real emotion. Acting is a challenging profession, because it's not acting.

So what does authenticity have to do with being rich? The Universe rewards courage, truthfulness and effortless Being.

Acting Rich is Being Free of the preoccupation with Money

A frequent exchange you'll hear between me and my wife:

"How much did it cost?"

Fred: "I don't know."

After a whole year of her asking me this question, I asked back: Have you ever noticed that I always say that I don't know how much it costs? Maybe I'm the wrong person to ask.

I realize that many rich people say it's really important to save money and crunch the numbers. But to me, that's not the law-of-attraction viewpoint, it's the work-hard viewpoint. One is mid-consciousness, the other is high-consciousness. In my view, money is not something anyone needs to worry about. If you act-as-if you are rich, you **assume there is always more** and you'll always be well off.

Acting like a Millionaire costs you $0.

34

Every Person, Place, Or Thing Has A Hidden Side

The last Live Course I did before global lockdown was 2019, Levels of Energy in Dallas, Texas (recorded on video, first two days available here). There is a scene from that event I recall the most:

I was talking about how everything has a hidden side, a shadow, a subconscious. Then I got an idea. "Even this building has a shadow. Let's have a look at the hidden side of this company". On the outside, our seminar location was a friendly and clean place. "Even this friendly company has a subconscious. That's the part it hides from the public".

So I walked over to a door I hadn't previously opened. It led to a storage room and boy, was it chaotic! Unrelated objects were piled up on each other. Some ancient piano, an old slide-projector (like the ones we haven't used in 30 years), dusty chairs, flip-charts, general garbage. It looked like a hoarder's garage.

And there was another door "that will lead us into even deeper levels of their subconscious", I said. "Should we open it?" The whole group yelled "Yes!". Emotionally healthy people are immensely curious. Apathetic people have no curiosity. Curiosity did not kill the cat. Apathy did.

The second door opened to a staircase. It was filthy, like it hadn't been swept in years. Paint was chipping off of the spider-webbed walls. Gum wrappers and soda cans were in a state of decay. "This is the shadow side of this company, the part they won't show to the public. Apparently they won't even show it to themselves".

I know what some of you are thinking: Does that mean this company has some unresolved issues? It sure does! There might be organizational conflicts between members or an apathetic manager or something else.

I mean no disrespect to that company, we all have a shadow. Every one of us. The shed in my garden represents my subconscious and it also needs some tidying up! It's got tools lying around unorderly, plastic bags full of other plastic bags (don't we all have those?), loads of dusty unused furniture. This article inspires me to clear it all out in the coming week!

I know what some of you are thinking: Will de-cluttering my shed, free something up in my life? It sure will! The shed, that no visitor to my House sees, represents by subconscious. "Unused dusty furniture" means that I have assets within myself that I am not using. Selling that furniture or giving it away means someone will benefit and I will feel lighter.

Every person has a public face, a private face, and a true self. The public self is what I call "social mask" in my book Levels of Energy. It is more or less authentic. The private face, which you show to close friends and family, is usually more authentic. And the true self is 100% authentic. It's who you are when nobody is watching. An integrated, mature person does not have a large distance between private and public self. Sure, there are always things that are better kept private. When a spiritual teacher speaks, nobody wants to hear about his sexual activities or his bowel movements (TMI), they come to hear about his views on spirituality. If the speaker is authentic, the difference between private and public manner will not be that big. The tone and expression will be similar.

There is a fine line between being authentic and being crude, impolite or inappropriate. Learn the difference. If most people in the world were authentic without shame, it would put comedians out of business. Much of comedy relies on expressing the thoughts of the private self. We laugh because we know it's true, but nobody dares say it.

If you wish to live in a more honest world, you must show more of yourself first. You cannot keep your own being in hiding and expect the world to be transparent and open. That's not how it works.

Here's the self-empowering point this article has led up to: Looking at a person, company, place, thing I am not only looking at the public face, I am also looking at what is not being shown. The public side is what is seen, the private or subconscious side is what is felt. That's why you can't hide anything from intuitive people for long. Luckily, intuitive people aren't that judgmental. If they were judgmental, they couldn't be intuitive, because intuition means receiving information from beyond the filters of judgment. Not being judgmental, they are not easily offended (the easily offended pretend to be non-judgmental). Instead of taking offense, they feel compassion.

Your communication is not only about what is being said, it's also about what is not being said. When a person is hiding too much or the contrast between public and private identity is too large, you get a "creepy vibe" about them. That "icky vibe" points to incongruence. You don't quite know what's wrong, you just know something is off. That's why I sometimes find it difficult watching politicians talk. It's nauseating to hear them say one thing, while I feel another.

Many people even feel there is "something wrong with the world" but they can't quite pinpoint what it is, so they come up with all kinds of strange theories. There is an incongruence between what you are being told and what is actually happening, between what you are seeing and being shown, and what is felt. But the good news is: The more real you become within, the more you awaken to how the world really works. The world and universe are much more amazing than most people think.

99% of all people are in for a real treat. The more real you get, the more weird the world gets.

Knowing that there is always a shadow and that the shadow is almost always hidden is a helpful tool. If you see a person over-emphasizing one thing, you know that the opposite of that is their shadow. If you can clear out all subconscious stuff and have nothing more to hide, you no longer have a shadow. You are then an en-light-ened being. One of the methods of clearing out the hidden self is to confess to your shortcomings, mistakes, actions driven by fear and anger. And if you are not ready to confess to others, even just confessing it to yourself (by writing it all out on paper, for example) brings it up out of the subconscious and into the open. If you stop wiping the dirt under the rug, you can actually clean it up. You can make amends or you can pivot your focus to the preferred behavior. If you have someone hear your confession, that person should be trustworthy and mature enough not to use it against you.

People who always find fault with others are hiding faults of their own. People who always express virtue are hiding wrongdoings. Knowing this, you can always see the hidden side of any person or company and help them integrate it. Integration leads to integrity.

35

The Weird Reason I Don't Support Human Cloning

To explain why I don't support Human Cloning, I first have to explain this:

Birth into this Realm   Birth into the Higher Realm

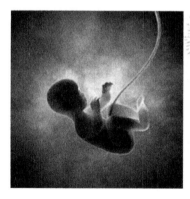 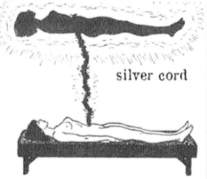

www.realitycreation.org

When we are born into this realm, we are born from our mother's womb and connected to her through the umbilical cord. Cutting the cord finalizes our birth into this realm. As long as the cords are not cut, we exist in both this realm and the pre-life realm, in my view. Yes, I do believe that the soul of your child is flying around your house many months before it's born. The moment the cord is cut, the soul zooms in to life on Earth and becomes linked to the physical self.

People who have had out-of-body experiences have seen that our Spirit-Self is connected to a Higher Realm through a **silver cord.** They have used this silver cord to reliably return to their bodies after their journeys through the realms. After we die, there is a short moment where we are connected to both Earth and a higher realm through the silver cord. Once the silver cord is cut, our birth to the **higher realm** is finalized. I realize this sounds unfamiliar, but if you want proof of it, you'll just have to learn to travel out-of-body and see for yourself. I have *seen* it with my own non-physical eyes.

I believe that our souls are created in a higher realm and, for this reason, we have a silver cord that takes us back to that place in the afterlife.

Here's the weird and spooky thing: Because Human Clones are created on Earth by Humans, they don't have the silver cord.

This is what the human experience is meant to be:

1. Descend to Earth.

2. Learn as Much as Possible.

3. Ascend back home after death of the body.

It's a simple mission. But a clone doesn't do that. If a clone is not here to learn and then ascend, what is its purpose? Slave labor? I don't know.

And if clones do not have an umbilical cord that was cut off and no silver cord with which to ascend, do they have a soul? That too, I don't know. But I doubt anything good can come from creating beings who become stuck in this realm.

Am I writing this article 100 years ahead of time? Maybe. Or maybe cloning is *already* being done. It certainly is done on animals.

If human cloning weren't real, there wouldn't be laws in place that support or opposite it.

Laws on Cloning

A molecular biologist at Princeton has mapped biotechnology policies around the world. Many countries with Christian traditions ban the cloning of human embryos for scientific research, while there is less opposition in Asian countries with Hindu or Buddhist traditions.

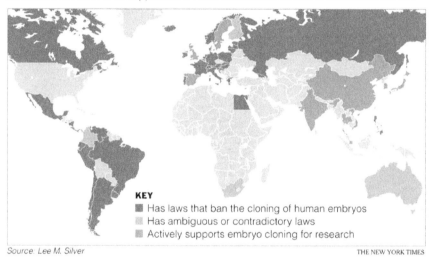

KEY
■ Has laws that ban the cloning of human embryos
■ Has ambiguous or contradictory laws
■ Actively supports embryo cloning for research

Source: Lee M. Silver   THE NEW YORK TIMES

We were already told 7 years ago that <u>human stem cells had been cloned</u> (article linked).

The broader issue is a "science" divorced from non-physical reality. I've been out-of-body hundreds of times, especially in childhood and my twenties (less so in recent years). The insights I have gained out-of-body have been practical. One example:

While you are out of body, you don't only see out to the front in one direction, as you do with your eyes. You see in a 360-degree circle in all directions at the same time. It takes some time to adjust to this and some people continue their frontal-view because the full-view disorients them. This has been of practical use in daily in-body life. I no longer depend fully on my eyes, but kind of "scan" an area with my awareness/feeling and pick up much more about what's going on than if I were only looking with my eyes. That's one takeaway of out-of-body travel. Another one:

There is no more fear of death. There is no wondering about what comes after. Death doesn't even exist in my mind. It's similar to traveling from one place to another. The advantage of that is a more enjoyable life and confidence in a greater overall purpose of things.

Our school curriculum won't even acknowledge the existence of a consciousness independent of a body. Without even knowing the *bare basics* of life, how can our Quackademics know the implications of cloning and many other issues? At the very least, the spiritual implications of cloning should be open for debate.

36

A 30 Day Challenge For Improved Mental And Physical Fitness

Incremental improvement is more stable than overload. This is a 30 day challenge for improved mental and physical fitness. Every morning, for the next 30 days, I will do the Clock-Meditation and Planks. Each day I will increase the time I do these two exercises. I invite you to join me.

The Clock Meditation

Sit upright on a chair, facing a clock. If you don't have a clock, use a watch. If you have neither, use some kind of timer. Put your hands on your knees and don't move at all. Do not twitch a muscle, do not shift in your chair, remain as motionless as possible while you softly fix your gaze upon the clock. Should attention drift away, gently move it back to the clock. It does not matter whether you look at the clock as a whole or some detail of it. On the first day, you look at it for 1 minute. On the second day, you look at it motionless for two minutes. On the third day for three minutes, and so forth. By the end of the month, you will be sitting still and soft-focusing for 30 minutes.

The Plank

This is a physical exercise, as shown in the image below.

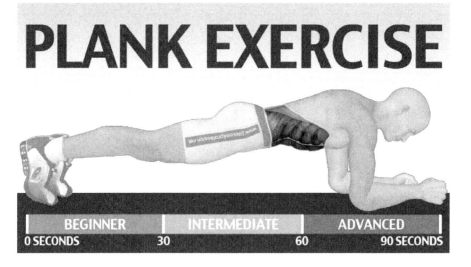

This exercises addresses almost all muscles. Beginners: On the first day, maintain this position for 20 seconds. Then add 5 seconds every day. At the end of the 30 days, you will be able to maintain it for 165 seconds. If you feel like this is more than you can handle, reduce it to 4 or 3 seconds added every day. Add to the time every day, learning to expand incrementally. Intermediate: On the first day, maintain this position for 40 seconds. Then add 5 6 or 7 seconds every day. Advanced: On the first day, maintain this position for 60 seconds. Then add 10 seconds every day. Or simply find a time that works for you.

Apart from greater mental discipline, calm and physical strength, the purpose of both exercises is to experience the value of practice. The lesson taught here is that never-ending improvement is possible when you choose tasks neither too easy nor too hard. That in-between-state is what creates flow.

I'll leave it up to you whether you start daily with Plank or Meditation. You can start with either or even alternate the two each day.

If you're taking part in the 30 Day Challenge, feel free to write about it in the comments section on my Facebook Page.

This may seem very easy, but don't be fooled. Implementing new habits can be difficult at first, as it breaks your old routines. But with every day, it becomes easier until finally it is normal.

37

Is It Possible For Others To Control Your Mind?

This <u>headline</u> caught my attention:

Really? Are there drugs that block free will? Can I become a zombie?

People of **personal responsibility** say that it's not possible for others to control you without your consent. You are the captain of your ship!

People of **victim-consciousness**, say that it's easy for others to control your mind without your consent. It happens all the time!

Which is true?

I say it **depends level of consciousness** (see my book series on Levels of Energy). At a high level, you *cannot* be subjected to outside control without consent. At a low level, you have given up conscious will and can be forced.

An adult person can sometimes go unconscious and lose their will. But before they became victimized from the outside, they, in some way, victimized themselves.

Quoting from an article on the Mind-Control Drug Scopolamine:

There are stories circulating that a chemical known as "Devil's Breath" is making its way around the world, being blown into faces and soaked into business cards to render unsuspecting tourists incapacitated. The result? A "zombie-like" state that leaves the victim with no ability to control their actions, leaving them at risk of having their bank accounts emptied, homes robbed, organs stolen, or raped by a street criminal.

…

… the compound is said to lead to hallucinations, frightening images, and a lack of free will. Amnesia can occur, leaving the victim powerless to recall events or identify perpetrators.

… According to a 1995 Wall Street Journal article, about half of all emergency room admissions in Bogota, Colombia, were for burundanga poisoning. Scopolamine is also present in Jimson Weed (Datura stramonium), a plant found in most of the continental U.S.

… The State Department notes on their website that scopolamine can render a victim unconscious for 24 Hours or more. In Colombia, where its use seems to be most widespread, "unofficial estimates" of scopolamine events are at roughly 50,000 per year.

And quoted from another <u>article on the Drug Rohypnol</u>:

Since the 1990s, Rohypnol has been used illegally to lessen the depression caused by the abuse of stimulants, such as cocaine and methamphetamine, and also as an aid for sexual assault. The so-called "date-rape drug" was placed unknowingly in the drinks of victims, often at a bar or party ("club drug"). Due to the strong amnesia produced by the drug, victims would have limited or no memory of the assault.

But: **Drugs don't have the desired effect in healthy, mentally lucid adults**. They could affect people who are already weakened. Apathy makes one suggestible. There are many who have had drugs put into their drinks and got nothing more than a headache and slight nausea. Maybe if they were beaten into submission or tortured, their Will could be overwhelmed by drugs. But only temporarily.

Unfortunately, "the Government" has done a lot of "scientific" research into mind control, hypnosis and the breaking of people's will. I wish taxpayers' money were put into more positive things. Prisoners of war, for example, have been subject to combinations of sleep deprivation, starvation, sensory deprivation, torture through sound or pain, forced repetition of commands, etc. It turns out that some peoples Will *can* and others *cannot* be broken. Those whose Will cannot be broken usually have **deep spiritual beliefs that supersede worldly assault.**

Some people believe in a "leadership", "schooling" or "management" style that reduces people's will, so that they can be "formed". This philosophy is called authoritarianism. Authoritarians do not want thinkers, they want workers. The world is run by authoritarians, because anti-authoritarians can't be bothered to run it. To counter-balance the authoritarian tendency, it's good to know your rights and never feel intimidated by peer-pressure, force or coercion. Develop your free-will, within the framework of respecting your fellow humans.

The answer to the question "can others control your mind?" is this: If you exercise your will, then others can't control your mind. If you do not exercise your will, then others can control your mind. **Simple as that!**

Things are a little different in childhood. A child will do things it doesn't want to do, in order to get approval and avoid punishment from adults. So it is easier to victimize a child and they should receive more protection. But even kids aren't entirely victims, as anyone knows who has heard a baby shout its lungs out until it gets its way.

Becoming a victim is usually a gradual, subtle process and so is becoming free. Every day that passes makes you a little more free or a little more dependent. This week I recall doing three things that made me more independent. These are *small* things, but they ultimately add up: I repaired my own watch instead of taking it to a repair shop. I chose to quit doing business with a company that mandated vaccines for its employees (**boycott** is an effective way to use your power for positive change). I chose to self-heal a knee-pain I had been carrying around for weeks from playing tennis (it healed!). Don't get me wrong, I am not against getting help from others and I am certainly not against community. Every one of us *thrives* when we have the support of friends and family. It is *too much* dependence that's the problem. If you don't want others to control your reality, then exercise your ability to think and decide for yourself.

38

Apathy Attracts Conspiracy

Twice in life, I was on the verge of signing a big book contract that would mass-market my books and put me on TV-Shows. But these contracts also included obligations for me to self-censor and be "politically neutral". These book deals didn't go through, because I'm not in the mood for watering-down. All these famous teachers already sound so watered-down, don't they? I know why they sound that way–they have contracts saying they mustn't talk about anything other than their narrow band of topics they published a book on.

On a similar note, I recently heard a well-respected doctor tell someone that he is not allowed to say that the anti-covid-vaccine has side effects because it "could cause skepticism". Imagine that! As if speech-suppression doesn't already cause enough skepticism!

Are we victims of censorship? No. A publisher has the right to their views, just as I have the right to mine. That's not "oppressing free speech", it's just a difference of viewpoint. Even though I didn't get these contracts, I am doing very well, thank you.

I was given a *choice* by this publisher. **We are always given a choice on how to act or react, though sometimes we pretend there is no choice.** The apparent choice was "get rich" or "have freedom of speech". But this choice is a false one–I can be financially well AND express my views. I don't need to choose between one of them. I don't need a big-time publisher so that I can express myself. The illusion is always that you need some person, group or external object for your success–this belief makes one susceptible to apparent victimization.

And the doctor? He "was told" not to tell anyone about vaccine side-effects. But he chose to tell me about this, anyway. And if he told me, I am sure he also told others. Even though he was told to shut up, he **chose** to speak. It's his choice. And I am sure there are doctors who chose to be quiet, perhaps out of fear. He also told me this: "*Never before in the History of Vaccines, have I been told not to talk about side-effects. This whole thing is unprecedented* ". Does this oddity point toward some kind of orchestrated conspiracy? Yes. Does it make me a victim? No.

A while back, I listened to a podcast titled "Catch and Kill" by the Ronan Farrow, while driving a long 8 hour stretch. I was able to finish the whole book in one drive. Ronan Farrow is allegedly the journalist responsible for bringing down film producer Harvey Weinstein.

In it, several sexual assault victims of Weinstein were speaking out, crying, traumatized. As much as I sympathized with the victims and despised the *creepiness* of a film producer abusing his position of power, there was an important factor missing from the entire long podcast series: **Choice**.

Weinstein had a weird way of assaulting woman. It was a step-by-step process. First inappropriate comments. Then inappropriate touching. And then, at some later point, outright rape. Some of the Models and actresses knew how to **exercise their freedom of choice before things got worse.** They quit working for him at the *first instance* of inappropriateness. Weinstein would say something like, "This girl will never work in this town again!" In spite of that, some of them went on to have successful careers, no need for Weinstein. But other women *chose* to put up with Weinstein's advances. Eventually, they got abused by him (and no doubt by others in his wider circle–it's sad so many others got off the hook). Some even *continued* to stay quiet and continue working with him after abuse. Some chose to sign "non-disclosure agreements" (NDAs prevent so many things from ever coming to light) in exchange for a lot of money. It is important to speak up and stand up at the first signs of lies or misconduct.

To behave in this way, these women first had to **believe** they didn't have a choice if they wanted to achieve fame and fortune. They had to believe they are in a vulnerable position.

Before you judge these women, realize that most of us think along similar lines. We put up with jobs we don't like "to make money". It's a lesser degree of the situation these women were in, but it's founded on the same false belief. *"I have to do something I don't like, in order to get something I like"*.

I've been receiving emails from people in Saudi Arabia, Germany, Israel and other countries telling me that they are "forced" to take the vaccine. If they don't, they become "second-class citizens" who are not allowed to travel, participate in public space or even go to their jobs. Some write to me saying "Fred, I don't want to take the vaccine, but I need to keep my job! What should I do?"

Well, perhaps you missed my response to that question in this previous article: <u>A vaccine against fear</u>.

And perhaps you also missed the 30+ books I wrote on Reality Creation, where I teach in meticulous detail that

You are not a victim. You create your own experience of reality.

This doesn't mean that there are no conspiracies. Bad agendas exist. Forced vaccination through vaccine passports is grotesque. However, it's still your CHOICE. You can choose how to act, react and handle the situation.

Back then, I chose not to change my views and got cancelled by a big publisher. But I did not believe that it would make me "poor", on the contrary. There are Millions of like-minded people I can do Business with, I don't have to do Business with this publisher. Likewise, if you are an an anti-vaxxer, I personally know a number of like-minded CEOs that would love to employ you. Whatever beliefs you have, you can use as a springboard to do Business with like-minded people.

In fact, people are *already* creating a parallel economy–such as private airplanes that will not require the vaccine passports that all the big airlines are requiring. The power is ours. Too much whining about conspiracies gets tiresome. **If you don't like the way things are run, build a parallel economy, a parallel reality, a parallel society.** Support a different world. Many of us are already living in a parallel world, mostly system-independent. Right now, I have access to several farms to purchase food from people I know personally. I have access to a private plane company that will take me anywhere. Why? Because I'm not a victim.

Loss of freedom comes to people who live in apathy. Many have lost their jobs. But this "mess" started long before Covid. For decades, nobody gave a damn about the political process, civil liberties and community. But if you do care, then snap out of apathy. The way out and up is to take charge of your vibration and to bring politics back to a local level and get involved. People are cooperating more than ever before. Sometimes I wonder if this would have happened without a crisis. Something intended for the bad, has been used for the good.

Remember this: It's all imaginary. A pharma company does not grant civil rights–they only imagine they do. A Governments authority is imaginary and only possible with your consent. The value of money is made up. And this particular pandemic is also imaginary–it only exists the moment you turn on the TV. If there were really a pandemic, you'd know about it without turning on the TV.

Since one year, I have been imagining something other than what I've been told. I've been imagining Success. Discovery. Hugs. Friends. Fun. What I imagine, I experience.

You are not victimized by conspiracy, you are victimized by your own apathy. **Wake Up.**

Becoming a victim is usually a gradual, subtle process and so is becoming free. Every day that passes makes you a little more free or a little more dependent. This week I recall doing three things that made me more independent. These are *small* things, but they ultimately add up: I repaired my own watch instead of taking it to a repair shop. I chose to quit doing Business with a company that mandated vaccines for its employees (**boycott** is an effective way to use your power for positive change). I chose to self-heal a knee-pain I had been carrying around for weeks from playing Tennis (it healed!). Don't get me wrong, I am not against getting help from others and I am certainly not against community. Every one of us *thrives* when we have the support of friends and family. It is *too much* dependence that's the problem. If you don't want others to control your reality, then exercise your ability to think and decide for yourself.

In fact, people are *already* creating a parallel economy—such as private airplanes that will not require the vaccine passports that all the big airlines are requiring. The power is ours. Too much whining about conspiracies gets tiresome. **If you don't like the way things are run, build a parallel economy, a parallel reality, a parallel society.** Support a different world. Many of us are already living in a parallel world, mostly system-independent. Right now, I have access to several farms to purchase food from people I know personally. I have access to a private plane company that will take me anywhere. Why? Because I'm not a victim.

Loss of freedom comes to people who live in apathy. Many have lost their jobs. But this "mess" started long before Covid. For decades, nobody gave a damn about the political process, civil liberties and community. But if you do care, then snap out of apathy. The way out and up is to take charge of your vibration and to bring politics back to a local level and get involved. People are cooperating more than ever before. Sometimes I wonder if this would have happened without a crisis. Something intended for the bad, has been used for the good.

Remember this: It's all imaginary. A pharma company does not grant civil rights–they only imagine they do. A Governments authority is imaginary and only possible with your consent. The value of money is made up. And this particular pandemic is also imaginary–it only exists the moment you turn on the TV. If there were really a pandemic, you'd know about it without turning on the TV.

Since one year, I have been imagining something other than what I've been told. I've been imagining Success. Discovery. Hugs. Friends. Fun. What I imagine, I experience.

You are not victimized by conspiracy, you are victimized by your own apathy. **Wake Up.**

39

The Cringe Exercise–A practice for Transcending Self-Importance

Go into a store an order or say something that has nothing to do with the store. For example, request a bike helmet in a bakery or ask about a stamp collection in the lingerie section.

The mind doesn't want to do this. It desperately wants to look informed, good, to know better and to be right.

This exercise is about trusting yourself even if you do or say something "stupid", even if you are unprepared. All is well, even when the mind is not controlling the situation.

40

Much of Reality is Make-Believe

How easy is it to fool crowds? Fairly easy. Just dress up like a celebrity and have two bodyguards with "security" written on their shirts accompany you. People will go wild.

The Video below shows examples of fake celebrity. Watch the first one to get an idea of how it works.

The interesting thing: There is not that much difference between real and fake celebrity. A real celebrity is also a human being, yet they are treated like "stars" and make people starry-eyed. Bottom line: What is driving people crazy is **not what is actually happening, but what they think is happening**. If you **think** you are in the presence of an extremely important person, you'll feel excited. But that sense of elevation in a persons only stays, if it's a genuinely high-energy person. If the person is faking it, then his assistants and aides quickly have to whisk the celebrity away, before it shows.

Human Behavior is motivated by perception of facts more than by facts. For instance, there is no pandemic. And yet, most people behave as if there is one, because "the media" told them to. I have received sharp criticism and cancellations for claiming there is no pandemic. From people who consider themselves smart and educated and won't admit they have been misled. It's daunting to consider that the whole world has been mislead. But it wouldn't be the first time in History, frankly. It's easier to fool people who think they are smart. It's difficult to fool the humble. There are thousands of health factors–getting oxygen, sun and movement among the foremost. Putting good things into your body is another. But these smart and educated people tell you that cutting off oxygen, sun and movement and putting bad things into your body will keep you healthy.

I've always kissed my spouse when she has the flu. Why? Am I ignorant of the fact that the flu is contagious? That might be *your belief.* But the **fact** is, that I have never gotten the flu just because people around me had it. I kept kissing my spouse and hugging friends and relatives, because I am immune to the flu. What makes me immune? Probably the BELIEF that I am, coupled with fearlessness. You tell me it's a "scientific fact" that flu is contagious. But that's *never* been my experience.

What should I trust: My own experience, made time and time again, or what "the news" tells me?

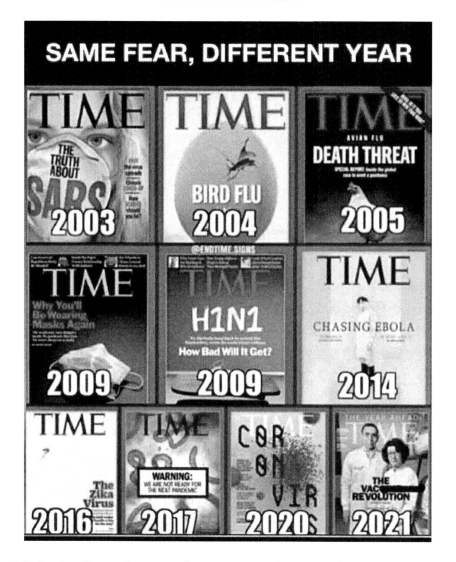

All the headlines above, made certain people very rich. It's the fear-to-riches scheme which has been running for thousands of years. But none of the headlines **resonated** with me, so I did not pick up any of these illnesses, despite frequent travel (including travel into danger-zones). All along I experience that thoughts and beliefs are contagious.

But enough of that. We can get into complaining about how easily people are fooled or we can use the **power of belief** to our advantage.

Just knowing that "monkey see, monkey do", can help you achieve business success. I advised a restaurant owner to have friends and family sit in the restaurant. Before that, the restaurant was empty. After people saw it's **already filled**, they believed it to be good and wanted in. Just that **one little shift,** changed the trajectory of his restaurant. I was his "last resort" coach before bankruptcy. A tiny change, and today his Business is thriving.

Much of reality is make-believe. Monkey see, monkey do.

Sounds cynical, doesn't it? But, it's not *all* make-believe. This restaurant owner is also a **fun character** and makes **decent food.** You can fake it till you make it, but you can only succeed long-term if there is some **substance** to what you are doing. Something **real** behind the packaging. See the image above? What does it have to do with this article? Nothing. It's just packaging. Putting someone attractive up to attract people is the most common form of marketing, used since thousands of years. Make-believe. But then this article better have some real substance. If packaging vs. content are too far apart, it angers people off. There are some who have deluded themselves into thinking they can run a Business on packaging and promises only, but these don't last.

I'm not a fan of packaging. That's why my books don't have a preface, introduction and foreword. I want to keep it real and get right to the heart of the matter. Nor do I pay for marketing. If I were more into packaging, I could probably sell more books, but I really prefer quality to quantity.

We live in times where much of what people think they "know" was made up by a PR firm. You'll realize that most of politics, news, information and education is without substance when it feels like you read a 10 000 page menu without having a meal. If something is of substance, then it makes a difference in your life. It moves your bank account. It sparks a feeling. It leaves you stronger. It makes you more forgiving. Or it's actionable.

We live in a monkey-see, monkey-do world. People tend to do what they see others do. It begins early on. We watch how our parents behave and talk, and copy their example. This has both negative and positive implications. The empowering take-away is this: You can stop doing and thinking things just because "everyone else" does and thinks them and start listening to your heart. "Set your Course by the stars, not by the light of every passing ship". Set your course by your heart, not by the noise of every passing trend.

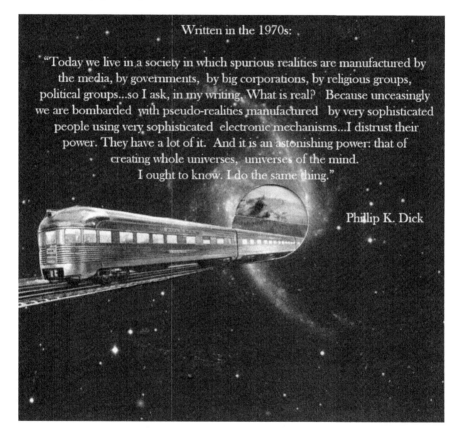

Written in the 1970s:

"Today we live in a society in which spurious realities are manufactured by the media, by governments, by big corporations, by religious groups, political groups...so I ask, in my writing, What is real? Because unceasingly we are bombarded with pseudo-realities manufactured by very sophisticated people using very sophisticated electronic mechanisms...I distrust their power. They have a lot of it. And it is an astonishing power: that of creating whole universes, universes of the mind.
I ought to know. I do the same thing."

Phillip K. Dick

41

The Power of Speaking Boldly

A well-liked manager got fired from his position. HQ advised people not to talk about it ("Don't get involved in the politics of the company, just keep doing your job"). The atmosphere the next day was subdued. Nobody understood what had happened, so rumors were spun.

The other day, a local man was found dead at the side of the river. There are three different accounts on how he died, but the police won't provide any details. Like the community doesn't need to know what happens in their front yard! So people go about their business, asking no further questions.

I do a one-month coaching with a guy. On the very last day, in the last 10 minutes of our time together, he reveals he was sexually abused as a child. Why didn't he tell me at the *beginning* of our session? We could have worked through it.

A teenager was brutally beaten by gang members in the locker rooms of a local school. It was so bad he had to be stitched up at the hospital. He was told by the sports teacher: "Suck it up". Nobody in charge said anything further about it. A gang member was said to have told him "not to be a snitch" or he'll get another beating.

Telling people to hush something up = disempowerment. Cover-up resolves *nothing*. It only allows *more* of the undesirable thing to happen. It leaves people bereft of knowledge, closure, and emotional relief. The only way to counter this kind of oppression is by speaking up openly and boldly. In so doing, you empower yourself and the people you are talking to. You make the world a more trustworthy place. Even if they disagree with your speaking up, transparency ultimately empowers everyone.

Speaking up can *appear* more difficult than staying quiet. But it's only a short-term pain for a long-term gain. Cover-up is a short-term gain for a long-term pain.

In the last few weeks, a student of mine has gone through one of the roughest patches of her career for speaking up. She had been in a hush-hush environment within a company where she was the partial owner. The secretive atmosphere had been getting worse. People taking money that wasn't theirs to take. There was backstabbing and whispered gossip. Having failed to speak up earlier, she hadn't even clarified her share of company earnings! She came to me for coaching on "mental relaxation" due to all the "stresses at work". But instead of doing the guided meditations she expected, I advertised for the need to speak up and be bold. All of our practice was only on that. Everyone in her work environment needed to come clean. And so she spoke up. Everyone hoped that her campaign for transparency was a onetime thing and afterwards they could go back to being sneaky. The subconscious doesn't like having a light shone into its darkest recesses. But her brave standing for truth continued. The co-owners in the company got really angry. Soon they threatened her. Funds were withdrawn and some of her partners jumped ship. A time of upheaval and uncertainty followed.

"I spoke up as you told me to, now the whole company is in disarray!" she complained to me.

"You can't carry the torch of truth without burning a few beards," I joked. But after the dust settled, the company was at a much better place than before. It had ascended a few levels in consciousness! The people left were treating each other well. Misgivings were communicated openly but respectfully (instead of keeping them secret and then exploding in rage later). Everyone was clear on their goals and responsibilities.

If you speak up *early on*, at the very first signs of trouble, then trouble has no chance to fester. Then, there is no violent revolution, just peaceful transition. When you have something to say, silence is a lie.

Speak up about things you see or experience in your immediate surroundings, work, or private life. When speaking up, it is wise to not only state what you are against, but especially what reality you *prefer*. Speaking out against things is better than not speaking up at all, but you are more likely to succeed if you tell others not only what you are against, but what you are *for*.

Exercise on Speaking Up

Answer the following questions:

1. When was a time you wished to say "no" but said "yes"?

2. When was a time you wished to say "yes" but said "no"?

3. Do you recall a time you weren't entirely straight in your communication?

4. How would you be had you been straight and clear?

5. What is something you'd tell someone if you were authentic and courageous?

Answering these questions a few times can help you **regain your voice and your ability to influence your reality**.

42

I'll Tell You A Secret About Donald Trumps Mother

Yesterday I provided an "Ask Me Anything" session. What surprised me a little is how many people sent me emails asking about Donald Trump! Even out of the spotlight, he's still the most dominant topic on peoples minds.

One email claimed that I haven't written anything about Trump.

My response: I have written about Trump, but you DIDNT SEE IT. The reason you didn't notice is because "the media" limits perception to either a "pro Trump" or "anti Trump" stance, with little question on who Trump *actually* is. My wish is that people overcome their perceptual laziness and look beyond what they are told.

Just *one* example: This is Donald Trumps mother.

Mary Anne MacLeod Trump

Donald Trump's mother

Mary Anne Trump was a Scottish-American philanthropist known for being the mother of 45th President of the United States Donald Trump. She was the wife of real-estate developer Fred Trump. Born in the Outer Hebrides of Scotland, she emigrated to the United States in 1930 and became a naturalized citizen in March 1942. Wikipedia

Her name is Mary Anne MacLeod. My last article, Fairies from Outer Space, was about the private beliefs of the MacLeod/Trump Clan. Knowing this, you can now re-read the article with fresh eyes.

Why didn't I mention this fact in the article? Because mentioning Trump would *distract* from the main point, which is to show how various elites *believe* they are bloodline extra-terrestrials.

Some of you (who ask me about Trump), didn't bother to read the article, because you wouldn't expect it to have anything to do with the topic. Why not? Because no news-media have *ever* featured the Trump Clans belief in extra-terrestrial fairy folk. One side images the Trump family as modern day Nazis and the other side crafts them as devout Christians. Thus, this whole stuff about fairies from outer space remains private and hidden.

I write this to inspire you to conduct more independent research on *everything*. One of the questions I received yesterday in "Ask Me Anything" was this: "Do you believe in the Afterlife?". My answer to that is "Yes". But I sure wish you'd done just some *basic research* on me. I've affirmed my belief in the afterlife in dozens of books and hundreds of articles and videos. Another person asks me whether I have ever heard of "the law of attraction". I already got this question last year. My answer is "Well, no, I've only written 20 books on the subject"..

These kinds of things truly amaze me because, by the time I write a question to an author I like, I've usually not only read ALL of their books but also every single interview they have ever given and even books about them written by others. When I read an article, it usually turns into reading several articles because I check other sources and references on what was written. It's never just "reading the article". I don't expect anyone to be a reading-fanatic like me, but some **basic** research can go a long way in improving your life.

It's a bad habit to take what you see and read at face-value, without questioning it. We think we "know" things because we have been told on TV or read it somewhere. But before we don't check, double-check, cross-check and verified, we don't really "know" a thing.

Maybe you "don't have the time" to research things–anything–more deeply. In that case, your goal could be to use *reality creation* and disconnect from the rat-race to regain your freedom, time and dignity.

I was speaking to a friend the other day. He told me that he had read the entire 10 page packaging for a medication, before taking it. What that showed me is his prosperity. Someone who has the time and leisure to read the entire packaging is prosperous. But one who takes their time to learn becomes prosperous.

43

The Mystery Of 1000 Years Missing From The "Galleria Umberto"

"From one thing, know ten thousand things,"

Miyamoto Musashi

Foreword

The purpose of this article is to show that *nothing is as it seems*. Drop your assumptions, then even this random building in Italy becomes an adventure. While my last article only took 15 minutes to write, this one took about 20 hours of research, wading through hundreds of old photographs, maps and historical archives. At times, it felt like I was on a wild goose chase, at other times I knew I was on to something. If you like detective-work and mystery as much as I do, you'll enjoy this article.

Missing Time

There is a French website of old photography from the 1800s, from private and public collections. On one of its pages, we find the following image of "the shopping mall Galleria Umberto" in Naples, Italy:

1 NAPLES. - Galerie du Roi Humbert 1er. — LL.

The photograph is said to be from around the year 1900, from a private collection. There is a horse carriage and a tram. Trams were introduced to Italy in the 1870s.

This is what the structure looks like today:

Notice anything?

The photo from 1900 says Anno DCCCXC, which means the "Year 890".

But today it says "Anno MDCCCXC, which means the "Year 1890".

---

890 in Roman numerals

The number 890 (eight hundred ninety) is written in Roman numerals as follows: DCCCXC

Decimal   890

Roman   DCCCXC

Convert to Roman
Convert to decimal

DCCCXC = 890

890 in Roman numerals

The number 890 (eight hundred ninety) is written in Roman numerals as follows: DCCCXC

Decimal   1890

Roman   MDCCCXC

Convert to Roman
Convert to decimal

1890 = MDCCCXC

By all appearances, 1000 years were added to the building. Or someone wants us to believe there were.

I took a screenshot of the original page, because sometimes such anomalies disappear more quickly than you can say "Fake History".

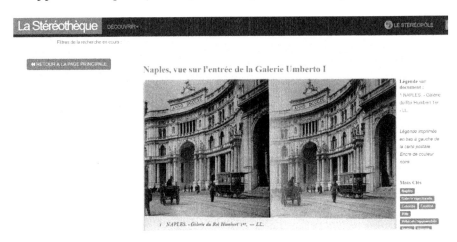

If the photo is genuine, it would mean this: Our great-grandparents were told that this building was built in 890. But we are told that it was built in 1890. *Why were a thousand years added?* And were they added to the building or to the photo? Finding that out is the purpose of this article.

Perhaps the makers mislabeled the building by mistake, then corrected their mistake later? That's unlikely for such a grand and expensive project and even less likely in the home-country of Latin, but not out of the question. I spent some time wading through old newspaper-clippings about the structure and found no mention of such an error. If anything, the 1000 years were added *quietly.*

But I didn't find *any* other photo showing the 890 either. The old photo above was added to the French website in 2013, donated from a private collection of someone named M. Wiedemann. Not finding a second source of the same info is normally a strong indication that it's fake. On the other hand: It wouldn't be the first time photos from private collections expose strange anomalies.

Wikipedia says this:

Galleria Umberto I *is a public shopping gallery in Naples, southern Italy. It is located directly across from the San Carlo opera house. It was built between 1887–1891, and was the cornerstone in the decades-long rebuilding of Naples—called the risanamento (lit. "making healthy again")—that lasted until World War I. It was designed by Emanuele Rocco, who employed modern architectural elements reminiscent of the Galleria Vittorio Emanuele II in Milan. The Galleria was named for Umberto I, King of Italy at the time of construction. It was meant to combine businesses, shops, cafes and social life—public space—with private space in the apartments on the third floor.*

The interior:

The Missing Architect

If it was really built in 1891, as Wikipedia says, surely we easily could find evidence of that. I looked up the architect Emanuele Rocco–and found *absolutely nothing* on him. No background, education, history or family. Even more bizarrely, he appears to have made only *one* structure–the

Galleria Umberto. Right then and there, I realize something is off. Would a completely unknown architect come out of nowhere and suddenly build one of the greatest buildings in all of Italy? And would he then disappear, never to build another structure again?

A few minutes after asking that, I found that Emanuele Rocco *isn't even an architect*:

Looking at Roccos Italian Wikipedia entry, linked on the Wikipedia page for the Galleria, we learn that he is a philologist. The page lists his linguistic works, but there is *no mention of architecture nor any mention of him designing the Galleria* (at the time of this writing). Surely such an *enormous* undertaking would have deserved even just a small mention?

So a guy who is *not an architect* and has *never designed any structure before or after,* comes out of the blue and expertly crafts a vast and stylish architectural delight? Possible, I guess, but very unlikely.

On the Italian entry for the Galleria, I read that Roccos architectural work was later "taken up" by another architect by the name of Antonio Curri. "Oh OK, there was a proper architect involved," I think. But then

I learn that Antonio was merely in charge of adding decoration to the Galleria. Why does Wikipedia list him as one of the architects, when he merely added a final decorative touch?

This article says in its title that Curri was indeed "the architect of the Umberto Galleria" in Naples. But in the article, he is no longer named as the architect, but rather,

"in collaboration with Ernesto di Mauro and designed by Emanuele Rocco, he took care of the decorations of the Galleria Umberto I,"

Alright then. If Emanuele Rocco designed it, where are the designs? Where are the building plans? I searched diligently, but have not found. Nor have I found any interview of Rocco or any public statement of his that takes credit for the building. I realize that, just because I haven't found it, doesn't mean it doesn't exist. But it's odd. Maybe it wasn't built in 1890 after all.

The detective in me went searching for places of similar architecture in Naples. I found one, and it's also a shopping mall! It's called "Galleria Principe Napoli", only two kilometers distance from Galleria Umberto. There are very similar arched entrances. It is claimed to have been completed in 1883, 8 years before Galleria Umberto, but it is said to have been built using a previously existing structure that was already standing in 1586–300 years prior! See images below.

The arched entrances of Principe Napoli look awfully familiar:

So here is a structure using the precisely same architecture and design, but claimed to be much older.

Certainly, if Galleria Umberto was indeed built in 1891, then we'd find evidence of its construction. I did not find any newspaper clippings that announced the completion of these grand structures. Maybe that's because Naples first big newspaper Il Mattino, started publication one year later, in 1892.

I did find one picture that is claimed to be of the construction of the Galleria:

The source of this picture is "Wikimedia Commons". There, the source of it is given as some *private persons Facebook page*. And I did not find the image on that page. I also found no records of who took the photo or when it was taken. Nor did I find *any* historical website that might have verified the image. Unfortunately, no surrounding landmarks are visible, so this could be a photo of just about any building site. The structure we see does have curved windows similar to the Galleria, but here it looks like it's already built.

In 1890, photography was a big undertaking. Anyone willing to bring all their photo equipment to a construction site would have likely shot more than just one photo and from different angles. But we have *only one* alleged photo of the construction and that photo is of obscure origins.

And here's the one and only drawing of the alleged construction that I could find:

Lavori di demolizione per la costruzione della Galleria Umberto I
Disegno dal vero di Edoardo Matania del 23 ottobre 1887

It is said to be from 1887, a few years before the alleged completion date of the Galleria. It has little resemblance to the photo above, but at least there is a known landmark to the left: It's the San Carlo Theater. The drawing looks like the area was under some kind of attack or fire. The adjacent buildings to the right look damaged and hollowed out. I found no mention of fires, wars or natural disasters around that time in Naples, except for a cholera epidemic. But a cholera epidemic doesn't destroy buildings.

A single drawing and a single photograph and no known architect–the evidence that this building was in fact built in 1890 is sparse, so far.

The Old Photos

The following is an aerial picture of Naples in 1887. I was excited to find it. In 1887 the Galleria wasn't even built yet, according to official history. Instead, the place was supposed to have been a pile of rubble and damage as in the drawing above.

If the Galleria was already standing, we should expect to see large structure where the Galleria today stands. This is what the area looks like today. The Galleria is now topped by a gigantic glass dome:

Obviously, the glass dome is nowhere to be found in 1887. So it would have been added later.

In the close-up of the old image, we can see a large structure beside a smaller dome. The smaller dome is of the San Ferdinando Church, which exists today as it did in 1887. The larger building beside it is the roof of the San Carlo theater, which is right across from the Galleria entrance on which we saw the "Anno 890" inscription. Pay attention to what you see across from that building.

Here's another close up of what the scene looks like today:

Notice the *statues* across from San Carlo theater. These statues stand atop the Galleria entrances.

234

And another close up:

Sorry that 1887 didn't have more high-res photography. But if you look closely, you can see an erect building (not rubble) and *the statue that tops the Galleria right where it is supposed to be*!

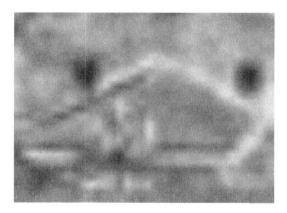

There are two entrances on this side—one has the inscription "Anno 890", the other says "Galleria Umberto". Both have three statues at their top. Judging from their shape, I'd say these are the figures atop the "Galleria Umberto" entrance. I cannot make out the figures of the other entrance in the image. Perhaps the other entrance was transported there from elsewhere later on, or the angle of the photo does not allow for a clear view.

A Google Maps view of the area below. For now, I'd like you to notice the location of the Castel Nuovo, an 11th Century castle in relation to the Galleria Umberto, it will become relevant soon.

So what is going on here? Why is there an old photo saying that the building was built in 890? Why can we see its top in an 1887 photo, when it wasn't supposed to have been built yet? And why does it appear as if Emanuele Rocco as the architect is a fabrication?

My guess is that Umberto Galleria was not built in 1890 but merely renovated and decorated, having the glass Dome added, among other things. Just as was done with the Galleria Principe Napoli. The photo below is from around 1900. This is an image made from the perspective of Piazza San Ferdinando (today called Piazza Trieste e Trento). On the left you see the San Ferdinando church. Right beside it, you see a building that seamlessly becomes the Umberto Galleria.

Strange but true: I could not find *a single photograph, painting or drawing from this angle, that was dated pre-1890*. I spent hours in search. I found hundreds of images pre-1980 from *other* angles. And I found hundreds of *this* angle post-1890. But the one I was looking for appears to have been erased from existence.

Does that mean that *nobody ever* took a photo or made a painting showing the Piazza pre-1890? Unlikely. Most images of the Piazza today feature both the church and San Carlo theater. Notice, for example, here, how the old 19th Century image is cut off in the middle. If it weren't, we'd see the Galleria.

All pre-1890 images showed an angle that didn't include where the

Galleria would be. For example:

The photo above is from 1880. I'd have needed the photographer to point his camera just slightly to the right to see whether there is a Galleria or not. How frustrating!

You can see the church dome and also the building to the right of the church, which becomes the Galleria. If you have a close look at it, you realize that the 1880 version of it looks different from the 1900 version above. We can see that between 1880 and 1900, the building has indeed seen some renovation work.

Looking from the other side, I did not find a single pre-1890 photo that showed the theater and what was across from it simultaneously.

Again, had the photographer of this pre-1890 photo of the theater tilted just ever so slightly to the right, this whole mystery would be solved. Here's what the theater across from the Galleria looks like today:

Normally I'd dismiss the "Year 890" photo as the result of some kind of photo-manipulation. But it would only take one single photo of San

Ferdinando Plaza or San Carlo theater alongside what is now the Galleria, to disprove this whole thing. Do you realize how *unlikely* it is that nobody bothered to photograph it and yet we find hundreds of photographs of everything else? This is as if someone deliberately made all the relevant photos disappear.

Instead, we have mysterious images such as this :

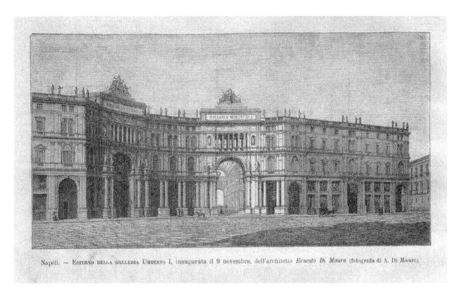

Napoli. — Esterno della Galleria Umberto I, inaugurata il 9 novembre, dell'architetto *Ernesto Di Mauro* (fotografia di A. Di Mauro).

What's so mysterious about it? If genuine, it looks like from a time when neither the Dome nor the theater across from it existed, nor a building continuing on its right side. In this image from 1890, for example, there is a building to its right, in the same angle as the Galleria:.

The theater is just a few meters across from the arched entrances. The artist of the drawing would have to be inside its walls (if the painting is true to life). The image says that the Galleria was inaugurated by the architect Ernesto de Mauro. If Rocco was the main architect, why didn't Rocco inaugurate it? Was it not written that de Mauro was not the architect, but merely a decorator?

The picture below was taken by Giacomo Brogi, who lived between 1821 and 1881. He died a decade before the Galleria was allegedly built. And yet here we see the structure's outermost tip, beside the domed church and again we see it in a state of disrepair, compared to the later version. The photo is evidence that the San Carlo street (the street the Galleria and Theater are on), underwent renovation.

I found a lot of websites that showed Piazza San Ferdinando in a side-by-side comparison, earlier and later. But every single one omitted an important detail. An example showing the piazza in 1870 vs. 1890:

Palazzo Pescolanciano e Piazza S. Ferdinando nel 1870 ed alla fine '800

The theater San Carlo, by the way, is said to house the *oldest* horseshoe-shaped auditorium in the world.

This is a painting of how the theater supposedly looked in 1830, quite similar to today:

Notice anything? This painting would seem to debunk my notion that the Galleria existed across from the theater before 1890. We find normal apartments. Of course, a painting doesn't prove anything. This appears to be the *only* painting clearly showing both sides, and I was unable to find out who painted it and when. The painting exists in several variations and also a black/white version.

Luckily, there is also a drawing, said to be from between 1860 and 1870, that refutes the one above. It is by the artist Antonio Bonamore, but it appears to be depicting an earlier time than the 1860s, rather, some time in the 1700s, judging by the style of carriages and the fact that Ferdinando square looks much different.

Across from the theater, see Galleria-style Arched Portals, three of them in fact. And one of them has the statue at its top. What to make of this? Again, drawings can't be relied on. This artist, however, Antonio Bonamore, was said to have done drawings that are "true to life". In that case, it lends credence to the idea that the "Galleria" entrances were already standing long before 1890.

There is also this strange painting that purports to show the theater after the fire in 1816:

It is not entirely clear which part of the theater we are seeing here. The photo appears to show an object across the street that more resembles the entrance of the Galleria than the theater. The soldiers are also oddly small compared to the structures.

Let's take another look at this photo. It is San Carlo street from the other side, with the theater on the left and the Galleria on the right in the background, is said to have been taken in 1890:

The problem? The Galleria was said to have been *completed in 1891*, one year later. In these photos, there is *no sign of any construction* work. The building looks finished and like it has been around for a while. Notice on the upper right you see a small piece of the Dome. Where are the builders? Where is the brick? Where are the carriages? Where are the tools? There is no construction work going on here. By the fact that sunroofs are drawn, you can tell that the shops are already running—*one year before* the alleged completion and inauguration.

The following photo seems interesting. The Galleria building looks like it's in a state of disrepair, as we would expect from it in a pre-1890, pre-decoration time. Even though it's only barely visible, the building does not look brand sparkling new here.

Finally, here is a photograph of San Carlo street in 1846. The problem? For some inexplicable reason, no photographer would simply turn around and take a picture of the other side of the street. Why? I found hundreds of photos of the area, but none of the spot in question.

The photo is by a Richard Calvert Jones. You can bet I searched every single photo this individual ever made. And I found several of Naples and even the right street, but alas, none that would show the Galleria.

Medieval Maps

Let's look at medieval maps. If the building is much older than we are told, it would have to be on old drawings.

The first map I found was on the Wikipedia page, Timeline of Naples. The map is dated 1572, more than 300 years before the Galleria was said to have been made.

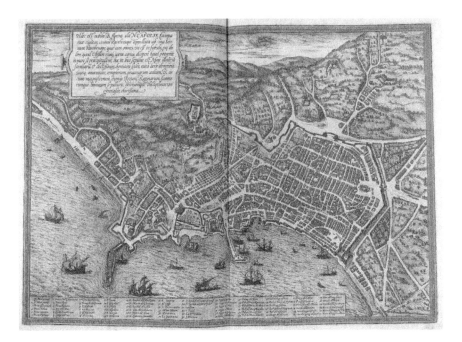

Sensationally, the map shows the curved street and heightened buildings where we'd expect to find the Galleria! A close-up will make it more clear. The Galleria is a diagonal line to the upper left of the prominent Castela Nuovo (see previous photo from Google maps for clarity). The theater San Carlo is not yet built, but there is a larger structure at the Piazza San Ferdinando (where you see the number 41 on the left), that is still there today. Nor is the church San Ferdinando built–which means that the artist Antonio Bonamore appears to have gotten it almost right! The only difference to today is that there appears to be a street between the two arched entrances.

In my view, these two taller buildings with the arched entrances are our Galleria Umberto:

They are precisely at the location Bonamore said they were, and approximately where they are today.

Another view from the Castel Nuovo:

This is a medieval gem of a painting. If you look closely–very closely–you can see just a slight hint of an arched entrance on San Carlo street.

If the arched portals were indeed built in 890, then we'd expect to find them depicted in old art and maps. And, we in fact do, even if vaguely. When I looked at paintings and drawings of Napoli that contained great detail, I always found them.

This is a map from 1815, where you see that San Carlo street is slightly curved, just like it was in the 16th Century and is today. Paintings depicting a straight road are not true to life.

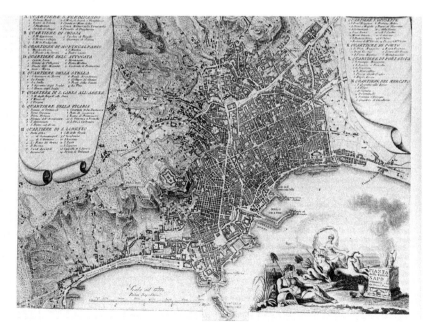

A close up:

Not all old maps and images confirm my theory. This is a drawing of Naples from 1522.

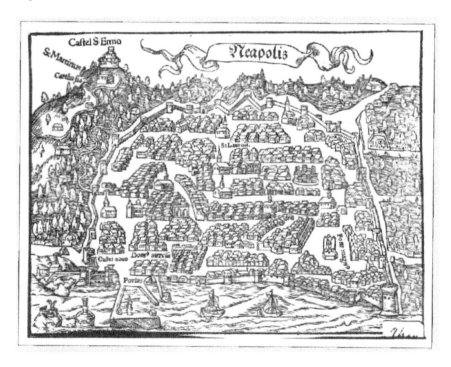

You see the Castel Nuovo, but there is no sign of any Galleria. Unless the towers surrounding the city were the archways. A closer look reveals that the tower just above the Castle does have an arched entrance. This 1493 painting of Naples seems to hint at such:

But they look nothing like Galleria Umberto. These pre-15th century drawings are inconclusive.

The Symbols

Taking a closer look at the interior design of the structure, I was surprised to find them lined with the star of David.

That's an odd choice to make for a building that was supposedly made as a shopping mall. The Naples of 1890 didn't have more than 900 Jews, according to demographic stats of the time. Or perhaps these stars are not related to Jews but to some mystery school involved in the building? I don't know. But I doubt that Italians of the 19th Century were likely to decorate one of their main buildings with it. I found no explanation.

The statues and the architectural style itself, appears to be classical Roman. But the year 890 would be approximately 500 years after the Roman Empire had fallen.

I will now show you Castel Nuovo close up. It was said to have been built in 1228. Maybe you notice something peculiar about it:

254

That's right. The Galleria Umberto, the Galleria Principe and the Castel Nuovo all share the same arched portal and pillars style of architecture. And yet, they are claimed to have been built at vastly different times (1220s, 1520s, 1860s and 1890s) by entirely different people. That's not impossible, of course. It's common to copy previous architectural styles. But where is the proof that a guy named Emanuele Rocco built Galleria Umberto in 1890? Where are photos of the construction? Where are the building plans of the architect? I couldn't even find a picture of this architect.

Conclusion

All in all, the evidence for the Galleria being older than 1890 is sparse. But the evidence for it being built in 1890 is *even more* sparse!

Why would anyone bother going to these lengths to make a building look a thousand years newer than it is? It's not that easy to fathom the motives. And I don't really want to, because then I'll spend another 20 hours on this article. In 1890, Naples is said to have had a lot of corruption and organized crime. It was also a time where "the great restoration of Naples" was proclaimed. In the hustle and bustle of all these restorations, it's conceivable that someone may have used already existing structures to take credit for stuff built earlier.

In short: *Take nothing for granted. Nothing is as it seems.*

44

When Is It Time To Let Go Vs. Try Harder?

Someone asked me this question, and it comes up a lot:

How to know the difference between when it's truly time to let go and give something up (like a project/career) because it's just not your calling anymore and you're just forcing it, OR when you need to just keep moving forward in the face of inevitable obstacles or feelings of doubt, fatigue and boredom with the sometimes tedious tasks needed to finish?

Short answer: Swimming downstream is more fun and gets you places more quickly. Swimming upstream makes you stronger. So there's a benefit to staying and a benefit to leaving. We usually see disadvantage in leaving and disadvantage in staying, but the heart sees benefit in either.

That said, here's how I live life, because I want both, I want to grow stronger and I want to achieve my goals: If 70% of my work is enjoyable, then I'm happy to push through the 30% less enjoyable parts. For example, I love writing books, but I don't enjoy the proofreading part. But I'm so excited about the book that I'm happy to push through that.

Another example: My marriage is mostly blissful, so I'm more than happy to work through the 1% of a time that it isn't.

The hard aspects need to be embraced (not resisted), then they are easier to handle. But if non-enjoyable parts exceed 30% the job. I've walked away from plenty of stuff and still do so up to this day. Staying with a company or spouse that doesn't treat you well most of the time, for example, is not "loyalty" its subservience. Sticking to a job you hate is not "toughness" it's a waste of time and talent.

Ideally, a person stays with a job until it's mastered and then moves on to learn something new, outside of one's comfort zone (and thereby grow). Unfortunately, most people overstay. They think that having mastered it, they are meant to stay there. But if there's nothing left to learn or master, it's time to move on. That's less comfortable short term, but better for your soul long term.

A question I usually ask back is this: If you had the courage and believed in yourself, would you still be in the job you are in? If the answer is "yes", great. If it's "no", then it's time to move on.

Another way to put all of this: Overwhelm is no reason to leave, but underwhelm is. Overwhelm means it's not yet mastered. Underwhelm means it's mastered and has become boring.

Imagine an escalator and a stairway. Some people choose to walk the stairs because they want to become stronger. Others choose to stand on the escalator because it gets them to the next level more quickly and easily. I'd recommend neither. Don't walk the stairs and don't stand on the escalator. Walk the escalator.

45

How You Can Help The World Regain Freedom

"I'm so excited to get the vaccine. It gives you a lot of opportunities," said a lady I watched being interviewed before getting her injection. *Wait, what?* I thought. *Really? A pharmaceutical company now gives you opportunities in life?*

Then I saw a headline: *"Google is now mandating Vaccination for their employees"*. Hm… wow. A vaccine does open up employment opportunities. Gosh. All those unvaccinated people will be treated like second-class citizens. Like in Canada, where the unvaccinated walk a separate line at some airports (in a year or so, I'll probably have to remove the word "some").

A day later, I saw a headline: "*The vaccines are ineffective for the new variants of Covid*". Aaah, I see where this is headed! A lifelong Government-enforced subscription to vaccines, so that you may have "*opportunities in life*". Hilarious. Or sad. Depending on perspective. I haven't even taken the *first* vaccine and they are already gearing up for the third one!

A student of mine told me that she arrived at work the other day and there were Government officials in the office. They had come unannounced and were vaccinating the entire staff. She was taken by surprise, peer-pressure was on, but she refused the jab. Her boss showed up and shamed her in front of the others: "You're going to get us all *killed*!" Her employer is now looking for a legal way to get her removed from the company. Colleagues didn't come to her defense, and she was the only person, among hundreds, not to comply.

I recommended she seek legal representation. Just because everyone else in her office is complying doesn't make it right. My wish is that this company and millions of others around the world get bombarded with lawsuits.

Nobody needs to sit idly by while the soulless, hive-minded crowds ("I'm not responsible, just following orders!") try to force their non-scientific and fear-based Covid-Religion on others. Many of us saw this kind of scenario coming from miles away. When they said *"only two weeks to flatten the curve"*, I didn't believe it. Why? Because the whole thing was *unlawful* from start to finish. No vote, no due process or discussion. Just outright and instant removal of your rights, for no good reason (did you know, for example, that masks are 500 000 times the size of a Covid Virus?). A Government willing to break the law once is willing to do it again. That's why, already a year ago, people were saying "just wait and see... they are aiming for forced vaccination".

Now, in 2021, some of us are saying: Wait and see, they are aiming for more than just forced vaccination. They are aiming for a universal, global and mandatory social-credit-ID. It's not about Covid or even the vaccine, it's about the remodeling of our society to full spectrum electronic control.

"Now, now Fred. That's alarmist! What's wrong with you? You used to be so positive!" someone recently commented. But I see it the other way around: If I need to turn on TV before knowing there is a pandemic, then there is none. Those who say there is a pandemic are the alarmists. I'm the one *calmly* pointing out why the alarmists use alarm (fear). It's getting people to act for the purpose of control, energy and money. In case you haven't noticed, the problem-reaction-solution scam has been going on for thousands of years.

"But how can you say there is no pandemic? I have a relative who got sick from Covid!" I hear you say.

OK. I also have a relative who got the flu. How is that a *pandemic*?

Dr. Marcus De Brun
@indepdubnrth

So let me get this straight in my head, I can have Aids, Chlamydia, Gonorrhoea, Ebola, Hepatitis, Meningitis and conjunctivitis.. and I can eat in a restaurant and go to the pub.. but if I haven't had a vaccine for covid-19 (aka nasty cold virus) ... I'm barred.

Seriously?

In France, Marcon was the first to eagerly announce that people would no longer be allowed to go shopping for food without a vaccine. Others followed. Then large corporations, such as Google, eagerly announced a vaccine mandate. That's not only forced vaccination, it's also an *unlawful* breach of the most basic human right–choice over your body. The laws of every country *prohibit* this kind of thing.

If there were any real journalism left, they'd be asking questions like this: *"Wow, I wonder why all of these "democratic" countries have suddenly and simultaneously all trashed their most fundamental laws and constitution without discussion? Might there be something much bigger going on in the background?"*

The gullible assume that all is well and that these brazen breaches of common law are done for public health and safety. But quarantining and punishing perfectly healthy people is not done for the common good.

A reader of mine (now former reader) said that I should focus more on the "positive, life-affirming writing" that I used to have and less on this stuff. But I ask:

What is life-affirming about passively sitting around and letting people of questionable ethics run the show? The very *least* I can do is provide a counter-viewpoint. Have people already forgotten the totalitarian movements of the 20th century, and how much destruction and deaths were caused?

Or perhaps they are not forgotten. Maybe it's a humans nature to seek authoritarianism when he's afraid.

An objection I sometimes hear is: *"We simply care about people. There is nothing wrong with caring."*

My response: If you care so much about people, then why don't you address the 9 Million people dying of hunger every year? Imagine putting only a small ounce of the attention given to Covid on Hunger! We'd have eradicated the issue within months!

Have you wondered why we don't fix that issue and a thousand other more pressing issues first, before creating economic destruction for a virus that has a survival rate similar to the common flu? It's because we have not been propagandized to think about Hunger, Cancer, Heart Disease, Suicide Rates and many more serious issues. Why not? Because Covid is not about Covid. And I am disappointed that so many people, including many who work in the field of consciousness, believe that Covid is about Covid. That's because people who say what Covid is really about, are quickly removed from public discourse and "social media". So all you get is an artificially fabricated echo chamber:

 State Averse
@StateAverse

this is disgusting, masks and social distancing should be in place till minimum christmas time at the earliest, the government are clueless, the Delta variant should be taken seriously and we should go into a national lockdown to prevent it spreading - my new favourite copypasta

17:20 · 05 Jul 21 · Twitter Web App

 CDM
@CDM0202

Replying to @PoliticsForAll

this is disgusting, masks and social distancing should be in place till minimum christmas time at the earliest, the government are clueless, the Delta variant should be taken seriously and we should go into a national lockdown to prevent it spreading

17:26 · 05 Jul 21 · Twitter for iPhone

 ≡+
@AzpiCesar28

Replying to @PoliticsForAll

this is disgusting, masks and social distancing should be in place till minimum christmas time at the earliest, the government are clueless, the Delta variant should be taken seriously and we should go into a national lockdown to prevent it spreading

17:09 · 05 Jul 21 · Twitter for iPhone

 Mano104
@Leedsmano04

Replying to @PoliticsForAll

This is disgusting, masks and social distancing should be in place till minimum christmas time at the earliest, the government are clueless, the Delta variant should be taken seriously and we should go into a national lockdown to prevent it spreading

17:18 · 05 Jul 21 · Twitter Web App

 •
@thfcsam_

Replying to @PoliticsForAll

this is disgusting, masks and social distancing should be in place till minimum christmas time at the earliest, the government are clueless, the Delta variant should be taken seriously and we should go into a national lockdown to prevent it spreading

17:14 · 05 Jul 21 · Twitter for Android

 SmithRoweSzn
@rowe_szn

Replying to @PoliticsForAll

This is disgusting, masks and social distancing should be in place till minimum christmas time at the earliest, the government are clueless, the Delta variant should be taken seriously and we should go into a national lockdown to prevent it spreading

17:23 · 05 Jul 21 · Twitter for iPhone

 Andrew Parker
@ToWalkAbroad

Replying to @PoliticsForAll

this is disgusting, masks and social distancing should be in place till minimum christmas time at the earliest, the government are clueless, the Delta variant should be taken seriously and we should go into a national lockdown to prevent it spreading

17:32 · 05 Jul 21 · Twitter Web App

 danny
@dannycn_

Replying to @PoliticsForAll

this is disgusting, masks and social distancing should be in place till minimum christmas time at the earliest, the government are clueless, the Delta variant should be taken seriously and we should go into a national lockdown to prevent it spreading

17:19 · 05 Jul 21 · Twitter for iPhone

 Jed
@Jed0st

this is disgusting, masks and social distancing should be in place till minimum christmas at the earliest, the governmen clueless, the Delta variant sho be taken seriously and we sho go into a national lockdown to prevent it spreading

264

You do realize it's your tax-money that is paying for hundreds of thousands of fake twitter-accounts, posting the same nonsense ad-nauseum, right? This is what the PR-Firms working for pharmaceutical companies call "creating a narrative". The whole Covid thing is a fabrication. The *appearance of consensus* is manufactured. Even so-called "fact checkers" are not what they seem, being sponsored by the very same pharmaceutical companies.

Such fraudulent "fact checking" messes with peoples ability to discern truth from falsehood. Not knowing true from false leads to an overall decline of societal health and cohesion.

If History shouldn't repeat itself, the totalitarian tendency must be identified, named and counter-acted through non-compliance early on. Otherwise it descends into worse.

I too have been told "*I'm getting people killed*" by not having taken the vaccine. I responded: "*So you're admitting that your vaccine doesn't work?*" The woman answered: "*The vaccine helps, but it's not a guarantee*". Not a guarantee is an understatement. The CDC says you can still get Covid, still pass on Covid and still die of Covid even if you're vaxxed. And you certainly still need to wear your mask and social distance after you are vaxxed. *Gosh, it's almost like getting vaxxed didn't make a difference.*

I've been witness to a lady who went to get tested for Covid *every week*. Then she got vaccinated *twice*. But she still doesn't go to public meetings "just to stay on the safe side". She's been working from home and living in fear for more than a year. Guess what happened? She got Covid! *Gosh, who would have thought that fear attracts what it's afraid of? Color me surprised!*

But here's an issue: This fear-person works in the HR-Department of a company I have done Coaching for. Upon learning about my views, she is trying to get me removed from their list of Coaches. I doubt she will succeed. But if she succeeded, I wouldn't mind, because I'd prefer not to work with fear-people. I never would have dreamed that I'd be dealing with this kind of nonsense in 2021. I'd never suspected that we'd be collectively referring to the unvaccinated as "killers". Is that really the way forward? That's what I call "the totalitarian tendency" and it needs to be pointed out without fear or shame...

... but without making an enemy of fear-people. I sent this lady a wave of compassion. That relaxed her. While she wants to get me removed as a Coach, I send her another wave of compassion. As she relaxes, I can explain my viewpoint. And even if she doesn't agree with me, we haven't dehumanized each other.

A bigger issue than fear-people, are the ones who run this *mass-media-machine* and know exactly how to incite fear-people. I am truly impressed with how effective it is. They can now generate a global unified message across all platforms. The unified message is blasted out to reach news-agencies, newspapers, radio, TV. Then it trends on Google, Twitter and Facebook. Then it appears in movies on Netflix. Then it is parroted by the mindless mob, without question. Then it is seen as "fact", because "everyone is saying it".

I recall when this whole thing started, people were wildly gesturing, explaining how the virus came from a bat in the wet-markets of China. They were speaking with utmost confidence. I thought: How can they possibly know this, with barely a few days that have passed since the outbreak? That's the power of the *mass-media-machine*. Back then I recall one lone person saying: "What if it's a bio-weapon from the Wuhan Labs?" but nobody took notice, because they had been filled (in-formed) with what the machine told them. Today, one year later, even Skeptics would agree that the Wuhan-Leak theory *much* more likely.

Daily mass-programming impedes one's ability to clearly discern truth from falsehood.

The bad news is that it's pervasive and unified across countries.

The good news is: As powerful as it is, there is only one small thing needed to disable the programming:

Trust more in your direct experience than in external authority.

Once a person realizes that external "authorities" do not have your best interests at heart, it's game over for them. Then, nothing that comes at you externally, is taken at face value. And so, in one instant, you've dropped all gullibility and can no longer be brainwashed. You're immune. I never got sick because I didn't believe I would. And I didn't believe I would, because I didn't trust others authority.

This started early on. A scene from childhood. My mom called: "*Come in out of the rain! You're going to get sick!*" and I instantly talked back: "*No I won't!*" and I didn't. That scene became the story of my life. My mom said "*Don't you talk back to me!*" but I say: If the belief-system someone is trying to impose on you is negative, then by all means, do talk back! Right now, there are too many cowardly people who do not like what is happening, but they are not speaking up! 9 out of 10 colleagues of mine do not dare speak up.

In an act of non-compliance, I stayed out in the rain, against my moms orders. After another few minutes, she came out and dragged me back into the house by force. While grabbing my arm, she once again shouted "*You're going to get sick!*". To imagine that parents actually believe they are acting from love when they are affirming sickness! And the moment she said it, I thought "*No I'm not*". And I didn't.

And what if I did get sick? Even then, I wouldn't give in to negative self talk. I will affirm my trust in the goodness of the Universe until the very last breathe… and beyond.

All of 2020 and 2021 I have been told by TV, Radio, Internet, Colleagues, Friends and Acquaintances, that I might get sick, but I didn't. Nor am I going to.

Just one little thing–a healthy distrust of authority–collapses the whole construct!

A healthy distrust, not a total distrust. Not all authority is negative. I distrust *fear-based* authority.

People say "But why would the officials lie?" Well, it's not everyone is lying. Most people are simply ignorant of the power of thought to create reality. Infancy is marked by dependence on external guardians or parents. The paternal protector or maternal comforter. If a person has not matured out of infancy, later in life they replace parents with Governments and Corporations. That's why it's good and healthy for teenagers to rebel a little.

Some are waiting for a hero to save the day. That's precisely the kind of thinking that gets us into trouble. There is no hero who is going to stand up for you. *You* must stand up for *you*. Last year I witnessed many who lost their Businesses due to lockdowns. There was no hero around to save the day then, why should there be a hero later? It is up to each individual to assert their freedom. I have. So I remain unmasked, untested, unvaxxed and unafraid.

So how can YOU help the world regain freedom? By these points:

1. Treat fear-people with kindness and patience (regardless of whether these fear-people are pro-vaxx or anti-vaxx)

2. Maintain your freedom and dignity in your own life and your relations.

3. Give people examples of why external authority is not always reliable.

4. Participate in non-violent protests or civilized debate.

5. Boycott the system.

6. Research and know your *facts*.

That's how you can help the world regain freedom.

And by facts I don't mean stuff you learn in the *mass-media-machine*. That's not science, that's PR. Just because someone dons a white coat, doesn't mean they are a scientist.

I've been using boycott since decades. For example, recently, I cancelled a phone company because they were sending me Covid-propaganda that I couldn't opt out of. The backlash against this kind of audacity hasn't manifested yet on a mass-scale, but when it manifests, it's going to be *legendary*! Years ago, I quit the private use of Google Search. If you don't understand why I would boycott Google, you're living in oblivion-land. I quit junk food. I quit pharmaceutical companies decades ago. I cancelled a Bank because of the way it treated a colleague of mine. There are only two negative companies left which I have not yet boycotted: Facebook and Twitter. But their clock is ticking.

If you think that boycotting these companies doesn't make a difference, know that they depend on *individuals*. Without us, they go broke. One person doing it, leads to another doing it and to another, until it becomes a trend. Finally, the dam breaks. *Many brands have come and gone this way.*

Protests should be enjoyed as non-violent events in which you align with like-minded people. If they go angry, they lose their energy. That's why your friendly "Government" have been found to insert violent instigators into peaceful gatherings. The energy-wave of aligned, peaceful protestors is powerful, but the shouts and vandalism of anger-people isn't. If the protest goes angry, Government feels justified to bring in police. They counter force with force and the energy is dissipated. But if the protest stays joyful, wave after wave of energy is created. Any Government that then uses force (against love and joy), quickly destroys itself. *Many Governments have come and gone this way.*

By the way—treating fear-people with kindness, includes not calling them soulless, hive-minded morons. I have done so in this article, to show that

I sometimes fall into the bad habit. But then I catch myself, release the hardness and remember the higher truth: Kindness flows from seeing the higher truth. The higher truth is, that only treating each other well, will improve society. Learning to trust your neighbor more than "the Government", will improve society.

46

Why Does Radio Music Sound The Same? Because It's All By The Same Guy.

I recently watched a movie called "Under the Silver Lake" (it's an OK movie, could have been better). One of its storylines was about *one* guy writing hit songs for *hundreds* of different artists. The main character in the movie broke into this musicians mansion. There, he discovered that many of his favorite hit-bands had songs over many decades, had been written by this one musician. Most of the "artists" were nothing but exchangeable shells.

If after the movie, someone said "Wow… imagine if that were true!"

I'd say: "It is".

Well, OK, it's not just *one* guy, but much fewer people than it seems. These few people, make 99% of the music you hear on the radio. I'll provide *just one example* here.

Have you heard of the musician Karl Martin Sandberg? No? How is it possible that you don't know the musician with the most produced hit music tracks in human History? Sandberg is a guy from Sweden. He's produced and written music of

Britney Spears,

Backstreet Boys,

Pink,

Usher,

Avril Lavigne,

Ariana Grande,

Kendrick Lamar,

Katy Perry,

Christina Aguilera,

Taylor Swift,

The Weekend,

Coldplay,

Justin Bieber,

Cyndi Lauper,

Jennifer Lopez,

Demi Lovato,

Selena Gomez,

Adele,

Justin Timberlake,

Ed Sheeran,

Lady Gaga,

NSYNC,

and many more.

We often hear the question "why does all the music on the radio sound the same?". Well, there's the answer. It's produced by this one Swedish dude somewhere in a basement in Stockholm. What a remarkable artist that is, but hardly anyone knows him! Even though he's been doing it across several generations of music-listeners, since 1985!

From this one example, you understand how only a handful of people are responsible for most of the popular music output.

You can find this kind of monopolization in other industries too— Amazon has a 64% market share in book selling and a 67% market share in eBook selling. That's enormous power over what the world does and does not read (this power was recently felt when Amazon started banning books by authors skeptical of the Covid-Religion). Google has a 92% market share in Search Engines. Their market control is not the result of innocent free-market-dynamics, but of Government-ties.

Many artists have little license over "their" music once they go mainstream. Britney Spears is a good example of this, she doesn't even have license over her own life. A team of lawyers and "handlers" are in control of her life and she just lost a court case where she sought to regain control of it.

Through the magic of PR, their lives look glamorous and amazing, but it isn't always. Some big league music producers say: *"I'll make you famous. In exchange, you relinquish your will and do whatever I say."*

This is why, in my work, I keep talking about "Success without strings attached", being your own Boss and creating your own reality. *Either you create your own dream or you will be used to create the dreams of others.*

Of course not all music producers and record companies are like this. Some are marvelous and support independent artists who wish to express their creativity. It's up to each artist to *choose* the people they work with, wisely. Every contract you enter, comes with new opportunities and obligations. That's true of any line of work. Some people who are starry-eyed, forget to read the small print.

Fortunately, the Internet has made it a little easier for independent artists to get heard and we are moving toward a better world where more and more people can speak to an audience directly.

47

Another "Virgin" Of Yourself. A True And Funny Story.

About 10 Years ago, in Coaching with someone who barely knew English. She pronounced the word "version" as "virgin". She was talking about "*becoming another version of herself,* as talked about in my books. But the whole time I understood "virgin". At the time it was awkward. In retrospect it's quite funny. An unedited transcript from our first session:

"Can I become another virgin?" she asked, meaning "another version."

Me: "I don't understand what you mean. You mean you'd like to reverse your reality and be virgin once again?"

"Yes, yes. Can I do this?"

Me: "Well, have you had sex before?"

"Uh…. no."

Here, I thought she misunderstood the question. In retrospect I see she must have been wondering why I bring up sex for no reason.

Me: "Then you *already* are a virgin. You don't need to do *become* a virgin."

I felt a little dismayed to have to be the one to tell her what a virgin is

"Yes, I want to feel I am already another virgin," she said in broken English.

Me: "Well, you are a virgin,"

"OK, I understand,"

By her deflated tone, I knew she was not satisfied with the answer. It must have seemed like I was simply declaring that it's done, like I had a magic wand. "OK, you are hereby another version. That's 300 Dollars please".

Me: "I feel you are not satisfied with this answer?"

"I thought you could help me become another virgin."

Me: "I'm sorry, I don't understand what you mean. *Another* virgin? Not the virgin you were, but *another* one?"

I was bewildered. I genuinely didn't understand what this whole virgin-stuff was supposed to mean.

"In your book. You teach it. I am this virgin and I become another one,"

Me: "Which book is that?"

"Parallel Universes,"

Me: "I don't say anything about virgins in that book. Or in *any* book,"

(Silence)

Me: "If you are already a virgin, you don't have to become another virgin. You have never had sex, right?"

Imagine how awkward it must have been for her, that I kept bringing up sex for no reason while she was trying to talk about becoming another version of herself!

"I don't know, I don't know,"

Me, exasperated: "You don't know? OK, let me ask you this: *Why* do you want to become a virgin?"

"I want to get my boyfriend back. He left me,"

Me: "You think you can get your boyfriend back, if you become a virgin?"

Imagine my *bewilderment*.

"Yes, *another* virgin,"

Me: "*Another* virgin? Not the virgin you were? Do you think your ex-boyfriend only wants you as a virgin?"

"I don't understand,"

Me: "Why do you think you need to be a virgin to get back your boyfriend?"

"Because he left me when I was this virgin. To get him back, I need to be another virgin."

Finally, after a long and awkward back and forth, it hit me: "Wait a minute…. you mean…. you mean another VERSION! You mean Version!!!! I'm sorry, I misunderstood the whole thing!"

In retrospect, I can see that she was making herself clear the whole time, if it weren't for one *small* mispronunciation. The coaching ended up aiming for not getting her ex back but attracting someone better. A reality creator doesn't cry over spilt milk because there is always something better, ready and waiting to reveal itself to those who believe.

For more on "being another version of yourself" see my book Parallel Universes of Self

48

The Manipulation Of Familiarity
And Attachment-Needs

What is the biggest secret of mass-reality-creation? It's the *familiarity principle*, also called *The mere exposure effect.*

Quoting from Wikipedia:

*The **mere-exposure effect** is a psychological phenomenon by which people tend to develop a preference for things merely because they are familiar with them. In social psychology, this effect is sometimes called the **familiarity principle**. The effect has been demonstrated with many kinds of things, including words, Chinese characters, paintings, pictures of faces, geometric figures, and sounds. In studies of interpersonal attraction, the more often someone sees a person, the more pleasing and likeable they find that person.*

Another way to say this: The song you keep hearing on the radio **is not played because it's popular. It's popular because it keeps getting played**.

Consider the last sentence for a moment. It provides a clue to how many other things work. And to how the world is run.

Popular Culture is neither Popular, nor is it Culture

Have you heard of payola?

Again, quoting Wikipedia:

Payola, *in the music industry, is the illegal practice of paying a commercial radio station to play a song without the station disclosing the payment. Under US law, a radio station must disclose songs they were paid to play on the air as sponsored airtime. The number of times the songs are played can influence the perceived popularity of a song, and payola may be used to influence these metrics.*

Even though it's illegal, record companies find creative ways to pay radio stations for mass-exposure of their songs. Thus, "indie" music bands, who did not sign on with big record companies that can afford to pay for airtime, must look for other ways of attracting an audience.

Regardless of whether you *consciously* like a song, repeated exposure gets your *subconscious* to "like" it in the sense that it's familiar and therefore feels "safe" and "cozy". Even songs you can't stand - if repeated enough - will have your subconscious create familiarity-feelings that will affect you to some degree. To some extent, influencers can override the conscious mind to reach your subconscious.

Modern "social media" works on the same principles as payola: *Organic reach* is prevented. Only people who *pay* for millions of followers, will have millions of followers. If silicon valley companies actually allowed organic reach, our "popular culture" would look very different. Many of our "superstars" would be unknowns and many unknowns would be widely acclaimed. In fact:

Popular culture is neither.

That means, it's neither popular, nor is is it culture. The popularity of the top 10 songs, top 10 movies and top 10 websites at any given time and whatever is supposedly "trending" is manufactured or fabricated, not organic.

What is truly organic? My work is, for example. In the last 20 years I've purchased close to zero ads and not paid for marketing. I've let the reach of my work grow organically, without any "selling" and "persuasion". That means my success has come more slowly, but it's also more stable, more independent and reaches people who dislike repetition-brainwashing as much as I do - conscious people. I'm glad I don't keep having to write books on the same topic and I don't have to mail out a shallow newsletter every other day.

Abusive People manipulate our attachment Needs

Have you ever heard of a case in which a spouse doesn't leave their abusive partner? Most of us have! Their thinking goes something like this: *I know this person. I am familiar and comfortable with this person. I am attached to this person. Leaving them and going into the unknown is much more scary than taking "a little" abuse. And maybe I am a bad person and deserve this abuse.*

It might seem strange to you, but I've met people who would choose bad-but-familiar over free-but-unfamiliar (see also: Stockholm Syndrome). At a low level of consciousness, freedom appears daunting, as if something worse happens if they dare leave their familiar setting. Some abusive people are skilled at manipulating peoples attachment-needs. Every human being desires the familiar, a sense of belonging, a sense of continuity. An abusive person seeks out weak people in which the need for belonging is strong. Then the abuser can get away with a lot before the person fights back or leaves.

Peoples need for familiarity, causes them to stay in relationships they don't really wish to be in, including non-abusive relationships that have gone stale.

Free Yourself from Familiarity-Hypnosis

Ask Yourself:

Am I staying in my relationship for comfort and familiarity or out of real love and joy?

Do I genuinely like my work, or am I only doing it because I've succeeded with it in the past and know it so well?

Do I really love my circle of friends and relatives or am I only hanging out with them out of familiarity?

Do I really love the TV-series I am watching or am I only watching because it feels cozy and familiar?

An example: I have binge-watched 16 seasons of the cartoon "Family Guy" a couple of years ago. But I don't genuinely like the show. How do I know that? **I have never watched it alone.** When I'm alone I don't watch anything. I've only watched the show with my wife, because she loves it and it provides a cozy and familiar context after our long day of work. I actually tried watching it alone once, and it elicited no laugh. But when I'm watching it with my wife, it gets a chuckle out of me because the person sitting beside me thinks it's hilarious, and emotions are contagious.

I've also never had alcohol alone. That means that alcohol is not my genuine desire. When I'm alone, one of the genuine desires I have is to learn something new, to read or to write. "Would I also do it if I were alone?" - is a question that helps you determine whether you are being fully **authentic**.

I remember how my wife got me to watch season after season of "Family Guy" with her: "Just watch a few episodes and then decide if you like it". See? She was using the familiarity principle. They also call it "acquired taste". I couldn't stand it the first few episodes but then "it kind of grew on me" and so then, I watched it out of habit. I think we watched an entire 16 seasons (back then) within just a year. I share this so that you see that every one of us uses brainwashing-techniques, even if innocently (also: I'm not saying that Familiarity as such is a bad thing. I am saying that it can be abused).

Creating a drug-addiction works the same way. If a drug dealer can get you try try the drug several times, they can build a familiarity. Even if you do not like the taste or feeling at first, a few more hits and the body starts getting used to it. Soon you believe you need it.

So yes, it is true that, to some extent you can "get into" and "learn to like" almost anything. But that's different from genuine attraction, joy and love. Things you *really* like do not require continual repetition and exposure for you to like or believe them.

Many have never heard of the familiarity principle or mere-exposure-effect. I believe that's by design. If people knew how it worked, they would realize the enormous power of mass-media and Marketing PR to create mass-reality. There are many things people believe, that don't even exist, except in their minds. If I'd list them all here, it would upset a lot of people. And there are other things that do exist, that are not believed, for the same reasons.

Why are some people immune to repetition-brainwashing? Because they've worked on themselves spiritually. Deep inside, they've called for truth. They develop healthy attachments and are willing to release attachment when needed. They are willing to let go of familiarity when needed, stepping into the unknown. Breaking your routine of action, activity, thinking and feeling every now and then, is a good way to prevent being manipulated. People keep asking me "What's your main teacher?" But I don't have a main teacher. And they ask "What's your primary method of reality creation?" but I don't have a primary method. It's better to stay flexible, without attaching too much to one path, method or source of information. The last three books I wrote are a good example of breaking routine. They venture into unfamiliar territory. I hope that your life too, sometimes ventures into unfamiliar territory. That's how you prevent the familiarity-effect of hypnotizing you into complacency. Stay awake.

49

The Power of Secret Giving

Give something **in secret**. Give someone a gift without the person knowing who the gift is from. Do someone a favor without the recipient ever finding out who did it.

When you use this spiritual technique, you are playing the role of "**the good Universe**". You help people believe that the Universe is a good place and good things happen for no reason. The more people believe this, the better a place the world becomes.

You can send some cash to a person you know needs it, without revealing the sender. You can pay for the next persons groceries and disappear before they find out. You can put in a good word for an employee. You can send a visualized prayer of healing for a colleague. You can clean your spouses car, without ever telling him or her. You shovel your neighbors snow away for them, before they arrive home and leave them wondering how that happened. You can list who you would like to secretly send some of your abundance to this year. **You can help people believe in miracle and good fortune.**

Things done in secret are normally bad. When someone hides, masks and deceives he is usually up to harmful activities. With anonymous giving, you are taking secrecy away from bad people and using it for the good.

The ego likes to take credit for giving. "Look at me. Look at all the good things I did". That kind of giving is fine, but it's not entirely pure. When *nobody knows* who gave, then the Ego cannot take credit for it. Exaggerated displays of charity and virtue are often done to cover up wrongdoing. Secret giving, on the other hand, makes the heart sing.

There are *too many* people around, waiting for someone to do something, some hero to step in, some savior to fix things. And there are *too few* people actually doing something, fixing things, stepping in, taking responsibility. You can be one of the **angels** who helps out in the background, is a positive influence in your neighborhood, community, group, town, city, country, planet, world.

Instead of just waiting for the Universe to make things happen for you, why not BE the Universe that makes things happen for others. That rapidly elevates your consciousness level to a realm where you gain more of the skills and information required to help.

Haven't you always wished for a surprising source of good in your life? Well, you can BE that. Then you cease to need it. **Everything you give, comes back to you by many times.**

Afterword

If you enjoyed this book, you will also benefit from Essays on Creating Reality books 1-5 as well as all latest articles at www.realitycreation.org

Frederick Dodson

Printed in Great Britain
by Amazon